AUTOBIOGRAPHY BOOK

THE RIGHT STUFF COMES IN BLACK, TOO

Dr. Thomas Mensah

One of the Most Brilliant Minds of the 21st Century

©Thomas O. Mensah All Rights Reserved

All rights reserved under international and Pan-African Copyright Conventions. No part of this publication may be reproduced or transmitted in any form or by any means, electronic or mechanical, including photocopy, recording, or information storage and retrieval system, without written permission of the Author. Any opinions, findings, conclusions, or recommendations expressed in this publication are those of the authors and do not necessary reflect the views of the organization or agencies that provided support for the project.

Published in the United States of America by the Author and CreateSpace Independent Publishing Platform.
ISBN 10: 1492802743
ISBN 13: 9781492802747
A library quality paperback book.

For book author appearance inquiries and interviews contact the Editor or Author
Sarah Klingenberg or Dr. Thomas Mensah by mail at:
Success Park Inc.
P.O. Box 54737,
Atlanta, GA 30308.
Lightwavecorp@aol.com

Cover Photo credit: Success Park Inc.
Book Design, www.eBooksolutions.org, The Publishing Division of The Infinite Streams Corporation

Library of Congress Cataloging in Publication Data.

As the famous scientist Albert Einstein, a genius, correctly pointed out, imagination is more important than knowledge

THE RIGHT STUFF COMES IN BLACK

Foreword

I was very fortunate to have met the incredible Dr. Mensah—a genius, as *Ebony Magazine* describes him—because as a telecommunication executive at Verizon Wireless Corporation, a giant in the telecommunication and cloud computing space, I know firsthand what fiber optics has meant to our industry and anyone who uses the smartphone or mobile devices to access our modern day internet.

Fiber optics' impact on the explosive growth of the Internet globally is incalculable. Fiber optics, one of the key innovations in this century, has brought us companies in the social media space like Facebook, Twitter, LinkedIn and helped launch search companies like Google Inc., Yahoo, and Amazon; changed the way news is reported and made our lives easier since we can now shop online at home and gain access to the library with a few key strokes on our computer.

The enormous bandwidth required for a faster and robust transmission of data, voice, videos, photos, and television signals on the Internet is due to fiber optics media. His work on smart munitions including the fiber optic-guided missile and nanotechnology products span many engineering disciplines. Dr. Mensah travels around the globe to speak on innovation and American competitiveness.

He is definitely an innovator in the same category as Bill Gates of Microsoft, Elon Musk of Space X, Vint Cerf of Google, Steve Jobs of Apple, and Thomas Edison as well as a strong motivational speaker.

The Right Stuff therefore aptly describes Dr. Thomas Mensah, one of the four key inventors and innovators in the Fiber Optics Revolution.

Charles E. Henry,
Vice President, Verizon Corporation

Dedication

This book is dedicated to the Infinite creator of this world and my family members. In memory of John K. Mensah my father, who taught me about achievement at an early age and allowed me to witness how he conducted business in his many enterprises; and my mother Margaret Mensah and brothers and sisters as well as my two grown children, Kim Willis Mensah, who is entering womanhood and Helena Michelle Mensah, my eldest, and my pastor and prayer partner, Reverend Juliette Richardson.

Acknowledgment

I am honored to acknowledge family, friends, and mentors along the way who inspired, encouraged, and taught me every stage of my life.

Friends from MIT (Massachusetts Institute of Technology)—Provost Ken Smith, Professor James Wei Chairman of Chemical Engineering now Dean at Princeton, and Professor Larry Evans. MIT taught me simulation and modeling of chemical processes. I salute Ms. Joan Robinson Berry, vice president at Boeing Company.

A hearty thank you goes to Mr. Ken Cannestra, former President Lockheed Martin of Aeronautical Company, and to Dr. Louis Sullivan, former HHS secretary, for serving on our Board of Advisors at Georgia Aerospace; to my colleague Dr. Peter Schultz, Fiber Optics coinventor and a mentor at Corning Incorporated, for his encouragement and belief in my talents.

My colleagues at the American Institute of Aeronautics and Astronautics: dean and distinguished Professor Achille Messac—a great mentor, Professor and Chairman Vigor Yang, Guggenheim School of Aerospace, Georgia Institute of Technology; Dr. Woodrow Whitlow Jr., deputy associate administrator at NASA; Dr. Norman Wereley, chairman and professor of Aerospace University of Maryland; Dr. Sathya Hanagud, professor of Aerospace, Georgia Institute of Technology; and distinguished Professor Ashwani Gupta of the Mechanical Engineering, University of Maryland.

Throughout my career there have been professors like those at Kwame Nkrumah University of Science and Technology (KNUST) in Kumasi, Ghana. I owe a debt of gratitude to Chemical Engineering Professor Henri Gibert, Montpellier University (USTL) in France, Professor Francis Allotey of Advanced Computing, and Dr. Francis Aquah, who taught me Transport Phenomena.

My colleagues who worked at the Department of Defense, Major General Jim Klugh (U.S. Army Ret.) and Major General Cornell Wilson (U.S. MC Ret.), Mr. Lloyd Resherd from Air Force Research Laboratory (AFRL), branch chief at Air Vehicle Design at Eglin Air Force Base, my colleague Dr. Paul Ruffin, program manager at Redstone Arsenal, and Dr. Isaiah Blankson, hypersonic research expert at NASA.

Also my appreciation to Dr. Takeshi Utsumi, Columbia University and Chairman of the Global Systems Analysis and Simulation Association in the U.S.A. (GLOSAS/USA, promoter of the Global Knowledge Centers Network - GKCN).

I extend my accolades to my business partners, Dr. Harold Jackson, MD, head of Telemedicine Programs; Mr. Charles Henry, now Global Vice President at Lightwave and Wireless Inc.; Major General Cornell Wilson (U.S. MC Ret.), Vice President Georgia Aerospace systems. My dear friend and colleague Fred Kessie at Lightwave. I say thank you also to Linda Jordan Director at Mesirow Financial and my Overseas Infrastructure Development partner, Steve Roth of Roth Construction Company in Texas.

Organization, presentation and first impressions were managed by my very able executive assistants, Angela Guzman and Sarah Klingenberg at Georgia Aerospace. My pastor and prayer partner Reverend Juliette Richardson of Ghana. Finally, kudos to my digital publisher, Keith Sylvester, CEO Ebooksolutions; the publishing division of the Infinite Stream Corporation, paperback copy, and Francesco Bozzano-Barnes for their guidance, focus, and tenacity in pushing me to get this account in print.

Table of Contents

ONE: Introduction 12

TWO: Fiber Optics Revolution 19

THREE: Formative Years 48

FOUR: Fortune 500 Industry Experience 55

FIVE: Entrepreneurship 66

SIX: Nanotechnology 76

SEVEN: Recognition and Awards 84

EIGHT: Service to Professional Societies in the United States 88

NINE:
Green Energy Revolution 109

TEN: Creating The World Success Park, Including The First African American And Latino Theme Parks 113

Eleven:
Recognition 120

Twelve: Technology Development on the Continent of Africa 123

Thirteen: The Power of Faith In God In His Life 129

Fourteen:
Prologue 132

Appendix:
Two of Dr. Mensah's Seven Patents 131

References: 134

The Right Stuff Comes In Black

ONE

Introduction

"The right stuff" is a designation that was used originally to describe the early astronauts who pioneered space travel for the United States of America because of their extraordinary ability to perform brilliantly in challenging circumstances, as those found in space. A movie was made to showcase their courage and performance under challenging conditions that require nerves of steel.

In politics, the "right stuff" can be used to describe political icons like Mr. Nelson Mandela, who after spending twenty-seven years in prison did not lose his vision and was elected an inclusive president of South Africa upon his release; Dr. Martin Luther King Jr., civil rights leader who endured beatings, attack dogs, water hoses while marching for civil rights and maintained the nerves of steel to secure civil rights for African Americans in this country and paved the way for leaders like President Barack Obama, first Black President of the United States of America, who was reelected for a second term under incredible condition of high unemployment, financial crisis and deficits.

In space exploration, The "right stuff" can accurately describe modern black astronauts like Dr. Mae Jemison, the first African American female in space; Dr. Guy Blufford, the first African

The Right Stuff Comes In Black

American Male in space; and Lt. Gen Gregory, the first Black commander of the space shuttle, NASA administrator; and Marine Corps Major General Charles Bolden, first black NASA administrator, and others.

In the military, the "right stuff" can be used to describe General Colin Powell, first African American chairman of the Joint Chiefs and later secretary of state; General Jonnie Wilson, four-star army general, now President at Dimensions International; Air Force General Lester Lyles, Materiel commander at Wright Patterson Air Force Base; General Daniel "Chappie" James Jr,, who was the first African American promoted to the rank of Air Force four-star general. He was another of the great Tuskegee Airman.

In the business environment, the "right stuff" can be used to describe Oprah Winfrey (who established the Oprah Winfrey Show creating a billion dollar empire), Bob Johnson (BET founder, who with Oprah made the Forbes billionaire list), and John Thompson (who replaced Bill Gates as the new Chairman of Microsoft Corporation in 2014-a Computer giant with Market Cap of $328 Billion). This same distinction can be said of countless others.

In the field of sports, the "right stuff" can be used to describe sports figures like Jackie Robinson in baseball, Muhammad Ali in boxing, and Michael Jordan in basketball. In movies and the entertainment, "the right stuff" comes in black, which includes Sidney Poitier, Denzel Washington, Lena Horne, Cecily Tyson, Dorothy Dandrige, and Halle Berry.

However, as we enter the twenty-first century where technology determines the economic strength and fate of countries (This actually differentiates rich nations from poor ones) with technological innovations that allow engineers to drill for oil under the sea several thousand feet below the surface, send satellites into space for communication and military use, and generate energy from nuclear reactors, solar, and wind sources, build submarines and aircraft carriers,

The Right Stuff Comes In Black

as well as connect continents with undersea/submarine fiber optic cables for broadband Internet and telecommunication.

Where military superiority on land and space is determined by technological advances, the place to look for the "right stuff" is in the scientific, engineering, and the technological realm; and here we find Dr. Thomas Mensah, a nominee for induction into the Internet Hall of Fame created by the Internet Society. This recognition will place Dr. Mensah in the rare field of Internet pioneers, like Vint Cerf and Bobby Khan of DARPA, the original architects of the TC/PIP protocol for the Internet.

Dr. Mensah was nominated for reducing the cost of fiber optics to the same level of copper, leading to the spread of fiber optics in the United States and around the world and making it possible to connect continents with ultra high strength optical fibers used in undersea cables. *Ebony Magazine* calls him a genius in a three-page feature article on who is who in technology, with the title "The Incredible Dr. Mensah" as published in October 2006.

Dr. Thomas Mensah's innovations have impacted many fields, notably energy, military/defense, environment, chemical engineering, aeronautical engineering, and electrical engineering. From fiber optics to nanotechnology, Dr. Mensah is a thought leader, technology leader—he is the "right stuff".

President Obama, who is also the "right stuff," used the Internet platform as his engine to raise millions of dollars and to run his winning campaigns, in 2008 and 2012. He relied on the fiber optics technology for this achievement. Facebook and all social media depend on fiber optics media for transmission of photos, tweets to anyone using the World Wide Web.

Fiber optics is one of the major innovations in this century because it has transformed the Internet into a faster and robust engine that reaches online users from every corner of the globe. Facebook,

The Right Stuff Comes In Black

Twitter, and others rely on fiber optics to interact with billions of online users.

If the Internet platform and modern telecommunication technology relied on copper wires, the main medium before the advent of fiber optics and the incredible work of Dr. Mensah and the pioneers at Corning, things will be totally different and one will have to rewrite history for our recent elections. The concept of modern broadband technology that relies on advanced fiber optics to enhance bandwidth (information-carrying capacity) has transformed telecommunication and the online experience of the average person in the country. This is critical to the Internet and all online activity.

The late Steve Jobs, cofounder of Apple Inc., another genius and an innovator, developed the iPhone, iPad tablet, and the Macintosh; while Bill Gates, software innovator and visionary, developed the Windows software for most PCs.

The iPhones like most smartphones and many devices would be limited terminals or devices if they could not connect to the Internet to reach over a billion people through fiber optics which provide and extend the reach and connectivity to all devices worldwide. Even cellular towers rely on fiber optics.

The cell towers have optical fibers on them, and in long distance communication the call from a cell tower is routed through fiber optics cable to networks to reach their destination.

One of the innovators of fiber optics technology that allows modern telecommunication and supports the Internet platform to permit over one billion people worldwide to communicate with each other is the subject of this book, *The Right Stuff Comes in Black, Too*.

The Right Stuff Comes in Black celebrates the accomplishments of the man whose dedication to Aerospace and Chemical Engineering, as well as scientific discovery, has made him a great example to students and professionals worldwide. That one can rise to the levels he has reached

The Right Stuff Comes In Black

to be an innovator behind the fiber optics revolution, one of the major players in the development and perpetuation of this technology throughout this country and the world. Inventor Dr. Thomas Mensah holds seven key patents in fiber optics, all awarded to him by the United States patent office in the short span of six years. He is one of the few engineers or scientist in the world who has worked for two of the most prestigious leading research laboratories in the world namely Corning Glass Works-Sullivan Park, well known for fiber optics invention, and AT&T Bell Laboratories, well known for inventing the laser and the transistor technology.

Dr. Thomas Mensah's work at Bell Labs was focused primarily on the development of the fiber optic-guided missile system, one of his main contributions to National Defense. His current work in nanotechnology has serious commercial and military implications for developing lighter and faster aircraft, space vehicles, satellites, and submarines/ships as well as land vehicles.

Fiber optics is the backbone of the telecommunication infrastructure in the United States and the world. Data, voice, images, and videos are transmitted over this medium at the speed of laser light, enabling users to upload millions of videos on the computer and transmit them all over the world. Google Inc. actually paid $1,065,000,000 for the purchase of the Internet start-up YouTube. Now this YouTube platform gets two billion hits per day, with viewership more than all three cable TV networks combined. Fiber optics makes this possible.

All search engines, Google, Bing (Microsoft), Yahoo, Lycos, AOL, etc., also rely on fiber optics media for robust and faster transmission of video and data.

Social media companies like Facebook, Twitter, and Instagram also depend on fiber optics to connect to their online users. Online video games like those from Zinga depend on fiber optics.

Anyone can access bank accounts instantaneously all over the world at an ATM because of fiber optics, and pictures can be transmitted instantaneously throughout the world due to the enormous bandwidth associated with fiber optics. The digital community created by the Internet and fiber optics means the library as we know it can be accessed through a few strokes from the computer terminal; one does not need to drive to the physical library. In fact, an entire encyclopedia can be transmitted in a few seconds.

In this book we chronicle the life of the chemical engineer, aerospace engineer, and fiber optics innovator, Dr. Thomas Mensah, who has been described by many people as one of the most brilliant minds of the twenty-first century and described as a genius by *Ebony Magazine* (October 2006). Dr. Thomas Mensah has been recognized by many organizations for his historic contributions to the development of fiber optics in the United States.

Dr. Thomas Mensah as an innovator is one of a kind in the engineering and technology environments. His work has impacted and continues to affect many engineering disciplines and industries including electronics, telecommunications, chemical engineering, environmental, defense, and aerospace.

He has demonstrated extraordinary philanthropic vision by creating The World Success Theme Park, which includes the first African American amusement and theme park as announced in *Ebony Magazine* 2006. His World Success Park inclusive of all races will help different races understand and respect each other while promoting peace in this century and beyond. This clearly demonstrates that his innovation and creativity extend beyond cutting edge technology and advanced engineering developments when compared to many other innovators.

His current work in the new field of nanotechnology and his quest for advancing innovative research means that our description of him, his creativity and extraordinary talent with the term the "right stuff," is appropriate.

TWO

Fiber Optics Revolution

Bill Gates, founder of Microsoft, recently in a joint appearance with his friend Warren Buffet at Columbia University Business School, was asked why he believed Microsoft could make such an impact on the world when he started the company. His response was that the microchip has been invented at AT&T Bell Laboratories and fiber optics media had been developed at Corning Glass Works, so he felt creating software to run personal computers in addition to these two revolutionary technologies could change the world, and he was obviously right.

Fiber Optics in this book is a general term that describes the entire laser based, optoelectronics and optical fiber cable technology and its many applications, which are used to support advanced telephone communication (voice), data transmission, video and TV signal transmission, digitized transmission of pictures, etc. on broadband Internet.

The Right Stuff Comes In Black

Laser pulses move data on optical fiber

Optical Fiber Strand

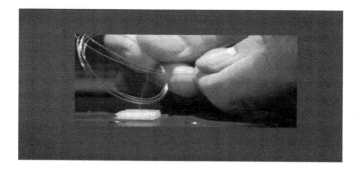

The optical fibers themselves are hair thin strands of pure glass with protective polymeric coating that carry digitized data by means of laser pulses. The mathematical laws based on Maxwell equations that govern optical media transmission are covered in detail in physics and electrical engineering books (The propagation of electromagnetic waves in dielectric media is a complex subject and those interested in such analysis are encouraged to refer to the engineering books and topics cited above).

In this book we present the technology in simple and comprehensible terms for the average reader who uses mobile smartphones and the Internet every day. The optical fiber has an inner core, surrounded by an outside cladding with a higher refractive index. This unique construction allows laser beams to travel along the inner core, while the principle of total internal reflection causes light to be reflected back into the core. Due to impurities in the glass fiber measured in parts per billion, the signal strength degrades over long distances depending on the wavelength of the laser and must be restored by repeaters (optical regenerators).

Even though Charles Kao, who worked at the British Telephone company, won the Nobel Prize for his theoretical prediction of the possibility of making optical fibers through pure or very low transmission loss glass fibers, the actual practical realization of fiber optics came from the scientist and engineers at Corning Glass Works where Dr. Thomas Mensah worked.

There are therefore four people who made fiber optics as we know it today a reality: three pioneers namely Dr. Bob Maurer, Dr. Don Keck, Dr. Peter Schultz, who made the first low loss optical fiber; and Dr. Thomas Mensah, who developed the high speed fiber optics draw and coating system. All of whom worked at the Corning Glass Works leading research center Sullivan Park, New York.

The development and deployment of fiber optics was not without its challenges. In the early seventies, Dr. Charles Kao has developed the theoretical basis for creating fiber optics, identifying impurities in glass as the key challenge in making a practical medium of fiber optics transmission. Dr. Bob Maurer, Dr. Don Keck, and Dr. Peter Schultz were the first to make a practical low loss fiber in the laboratory at Corning Glass Works. Dr. Thomas Mensah developed scalable high speed manufacturing draw and coating techniques to make fiber optics cost effective.

In fiber optics manufacturing, the chemicals silicon tetrachloride, and dopants germanium tetrachloride are deposited via a CVD (Chemical Vapor Deposition) process on a rotating mandrel, a few centimeters in diameter and 4 to 7 ft. long. The core of the fiber is mainly germanium tetrachloride. In a single mode fiber the profile is a step function while in multimode fibers the profile is curved.

The Right Stuff Comes In Black

There are three processes used worldwide for this initial deposition step in optical fiber manufacturing namely Outside Vapor Deposition (OVD) developed by Corning, the Inside Deposition Process (IVD) developed by AT&T Bell Laboratories, and Axial Deposition Process AVD developed in Japan.

The first two processes are shown below. The starting chemicals are entrained in a stream of oxygen to the burner, which traverses back and forth while heating the deposition surface which is rotating on a mechanical lathe. The flow rates of the chemicals are controlled using a computer system. The process parameters are burner passes, rotation speed, deposition temperature measured by infrared cameras and flow rates of the chemicals. A closed loop control system run by the computer software can be implemented to insure quality of the Deposition process.

Dr. Peter Schultz and the other coinventors conceived and developed these processes in Sullivan Park. The heat and mass transfer analysis of the process can be found in engineering books including the *Fiber Optics Engineering Book* edited by Dr. Thomas Mensah in 1987.

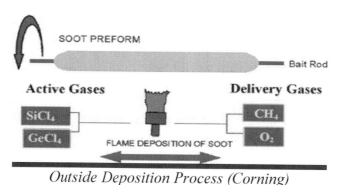

Outside Deposition Process (Corning)

The Right Stuff Comes In Black

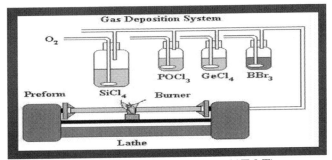

Inside Deposition Process (AT&T)

In the Japanese process, deposition occurs at the end of a substrate that is moved axially upwards during deposition. *Regardless of the type of the deposition process employed in this first step, the glass must be drawn and coated or transformed into a useful optical fiber suitable for data, voice, and video transmission to support the Internet and telephone calls.*

After the deposition process the deposited glass soot is consolidated in a high temperature furnace by a process called sintering, which transforms the soft glass sooth (This has the texture of snowflakes) to a transparent solid glass cylinder. The surface of glass is etched with acids to remove impurities, dried, *and transported to the second and very important stage of the manufacturing—the Draw and Coating Process.*

The solid glass cylinder is installed in the Fiber Optics Draw furnace where it is heated to 2000 degrees Fahrenheit and pulled like toffee using the take off spool several meters below. The glass passes through a cooling chamber, its diameter monitored by a laser system before entering the first coating applicator followed by a second coating applicator.

In each applicator a thin film of protective coating is applied circumferentially before entering the ultraviolet curing system located below each applicator. As the coated fiber traverses the ultraviolet curing system, the liquid coating cures instantaneously because of the photo initiators in it, before the fiber is taken up by the spool. The

The Right Stuff Comes In Black

coating protects the glass from breakage. The entire draw and coating system is shown in the schematic diagram shown below.

For over fifteen years the ability to manufacture fiber optics economically for it to replace copper wires was hindered by the drawing and simultaneous coating step. The delicate glass fibers broke anytime manufacturing speeds were pushed beyond two meters a second.

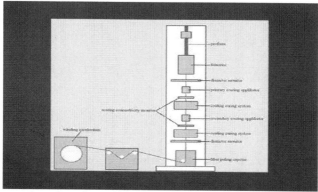

Protective Coating allow the optical fiber to bend easily

Dr. Thomas Mensah, then a young chemical engineer at Corning Glass Works, came up with a series of inventions that solved this worldwide problem at the age of thirty-five.

His first patent allowed fiber optics to be manufactured at ten times the rate limiting speed that is twenty meters per second without glass breakage. He was awarded the Individual Outstanding Contributor Award (IOC) by Corning Glass Works and a cash prize of $10,000 in 1985. Peter Schultz, one of the original fiber optics pioneers, commented that solving this problem was critical for large scale low cost manufacturing of fiber optics throughout the world.

At the age of thirty-five years when he received his first patent that solved this worldwide problem in fiber optics manufacturing, he was the only black among the four fiber optics pioneers, namely Peter Schultz, Don Keck, Bob Maurer, and Thomas Mensah.

This innovation in fiber optics at the manufacturing level based on his pioneering inventions put Corning Glass Works and the United States in the leading position worldwide in the deployment of fiber optics because the cost of fiber optics which was $1 per meter has been dramatically reduced to ten cents per meter, the same cost as copper. This made it economical to replace all copper wires and cables in the United States with fiber optics. This development also made Corning and AT&T worldwide leaders in the fiber optics communication and expanded the entire U.S. economy tremendously.

Impact of Dr. Mensah on the Internet, Cell Phones and Cable TV

The inventions of Dr. Thomas Mensah and the deployment of fiber optics throughout the country coincided with the advent of the Internet, which in the early eighties was at its infancy. Because of the limited bandwidth associated with copper cables, the Internet could not take off rapidly since transmitting pictures took several hours. The logical development of fiber optics as a replacement of copper wires led to the explosive growth of the Internet platform in the United States and the world over because now the full potential of the Internet platform can be exploited.

Wireless communication also benefited because now from the proverbial cell tower, one can tie into the fiber optics backbone (network buried in the ground and under the sea) to make long distance calls using the cell phone across the country and even to Europe, China, or Japan.

Dr. Mensah also received additional patents for "noncontact" monitoring of tension in a moving fiber based on a laser system, a novel optical fiber ultraviolet curing system, and a system that produces bubble-free and defect-free optical fiber useful for submarine cable and missile guidance applications. These patents together allowed ultra-high speed manufacturing of optical fibers, up to fifty meters per second leading to low cost optical fibers to support the growing Internet platform worldwide. A robust and faster Internet is now possible because of these innovations by Dr. Thomas Mensah.

The Right Stuff Comes In Black

Laser Pulses On Optical Fiber

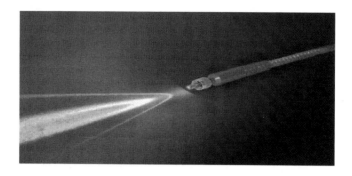

Broadband is now a reality because bandwidth limitations have been removed and pictures, video, etc., can all be transmitted over fiber optics. Cable television can now be bundled with Internet and telephone transmission because with fiber to the home and offices, high definition TV signals can be transmitted directly to the average American as COMCAST does with Xfinity and AT&T does with U-verse, as well as other cable companies in this country and throughout the world.

The digitized world through fiber optics now provides the ability to reach millions of people for political campaigns and to raise substantial amount of political contributions using the Internet. This obviously gave President Obama superior advantage over his competitors. Future potential political candidates are now featuring the internet and fiber optics technology in their campaign strategy, whenever they use Twitter, Facebook, etc., to raise money and connect with grass root campaigns.

The Internet now connects over one billion people because of fiber optics. Dr. Mensah's innovation produced low cost defect-free high strength optical fibers that can be used in submarine cables. These optical fibers must not only survive the cabling operations without breakage or loss of excellent laser transmission quality, but also be strong enough for submarine/undersea applications.

The Right Stuff Comes In Black

In these days fiber optic cables are used to connect continents and countries notably United States, Europe, China, Japan, Russia, Australia, Middle East, South America, and recently Africa. Internet transmission using lasers traveling over the fiber optics media can now carry, voice, data, pictures, video at the speed of Light. There are twenty-four billion e-mails sent per day, replacing the traditional slow paper mail. This is what explains the current challenges facing traditional post offices as they compete with electronic mails.

Interactivity

Because of Twitter and other social media platforms and fiber optics technology, there is interactivity between television viewers and online users and television programmers or content developers. This interactivity is important to content developers because they can receive instantaneous feedback as to what programs the Internet users and TV audience love so that advertising can be targeted. The huge advertising dollars drives the revenues of Internet companies like Google, Facebook, Twitter, Yahoo, and Microsoft as well as TV companies.

Because of interactivity, news broadcasters, musicians, sports and political figures, entertainers as well as many movie stars can communicate with audiences and fans all over the globe. Twitter has surpassed Facebook on mobile advertising revenues. Twitter, the leader in this field, filed documents to do an IPO recently. The Twitter IPO was more successful than Facebook IPO, raising $42,000,000,000 in the first day. The initial stock price was up 73 percent at its first day of opening. Fiber optic media makes all interactivity on Twitter possible.

Mobile Devices and Internet Applications

The mobile space is transforming the Internet as we know it because through smartphones, tablets, e-readers, and laptops, online users are accessing the internet anywhere and at any time. The smartphone in users' pockets can easily permit access to Internet for one to get Google maps for directions, do online dating, do online shopping, control home appliances from work or the car, make reservations at restaurants, etc. All these access require robust and faster Internet broadband transmission through fiber optics.

Mobile is a game changer in the Internet space and all Internet companies are racing to compete and be relevant in this arena. This includes Google, Yahoo, Facebook, Microsoft, Apple Inc., Samsung, etc. Jeff Bezos and Amazon are taking this mobile challenge very seriously. They are developing a smartphone with 3-D screens. Television news and programs can now be viewed live on mobile devices like tablets, smartphones including sports content, etc. Fiber optics is the transmission media for live streaming of shows, movies, and television programs.

Wearable Computing

Telemedicine applications via smartphones and mobile devices are expanding especially with developments of advanced sensing techniques. In the future the smartwatch may have functions of digital access to the Internet, sensing and monitoring health, EKG, data from the skin of a person, and transmitting these data and vital signs by wireless and fiber optics several miles away to his doctor. Google Inc. is developing a smart contact lens that has embedded sensors that will measure glucose level in tears, a major development for Diabetes patients.

Telecardiology is now here! The cover of the steering wheel in your car will contain sensors that can monitor your vital signs through your palm as you drive on the highway. Football players will have such sensors in their helmets to monitor severe concussion during a game. Boxing headgear will also be usefully equipped with this wearable computing technology and data displayed on screens of mobile devices for doctors and coaches to use.

My former employer, Corning Inc., is playing a key role in developing thin flexible glass for wearable computing. When integrated with sensors, this thin flexible glass can have many applications.

Google Glass and Apple watch smartphones will look more fashionable and could become mainstream when introduced into the market. Wearable computing market may reach over ten billion in 2015.

Samsung Electronics Company is now the world's largest smartphone maker. The company has also released the Galaxy Gear, its first digital smartwatch at a trade show in Berlin Germany in September 2013, racing ahead of Apple with this introduction.

This smartwatch will run apps and work with Samsung family of smartphones like Galaxy 3. The Galaxy Gear features a 1.9 megapixel camera, embedded in the strap and a built in speaker so users can make hands free calls.

Sony Corporation has also unveiled an Android operating system based smartwatch which will start selling in September 2013.

Qualcomm Inc., a wireless chip maker will ship a new smartphone, the "Toq," based on Android operating system to work with Google Corporation's family of smartphones in late 2013.

This innovative smartwatch uses the Mirasol technology with screens that require less power but can render full motion video. The watch works with ambient light, making it easier to see even when used in sunlight outdoors. A push of a button allows one to change screens.

Some smartwatch designs have sixty preloaded apps including a step-counting pedometer. These devices have touch screen and voice command capabilities.

This first generation of smartwatches is limited to working with the family of smartphones of each supplier, in this case, communicating directly with the handset. One benefit of this smartwatch technology is to let a user check their calendar without switching from a phone conversation or browsing session. The smartwatch therefore becomes an important accessory to the smartphone in this case. The battery life for these smartwatches which will sell around $300 is limited to three to seven days.

Dr. Thomas Mensah and his team at Lightwave and Wireless are working on nanotechnoloy based batteries that can extend the battery life even to six months or a year.

Mobile applications and smartphone applications have caught everyone by surprise and professional social media company CEO Jeff Weiner of LinkedIn Corporation is moving rapidly in this area to reach a higher level of engagement. LinkedIn, which just celebrated its tenth year, is a professional social media platform which has over two hundred million users. They focus on hiring and professional networking. LinkedIn has recently purchased Pulse to accelerate its entry into the mobile space. Its Post IPO performance has been more spectacular than other social media companies like Facebook, Groupon, Zinga and Yelp.

LinkedIn Corporation is one of the leaders when it comes to protecting online users' private information. Such private information is not shared as it occurs in other social media platforms and, therefore, many corporate executives are on the LinkedIn platform. LinkedIn is also developing its publishing platforms and features successful business moguls like Sir Richard Branson and political leaders like President Obama to interact with its online users.

Facebook and all social media networks are facing challenges in the transition to the rapidly expanding "mobile space." They are paying billions of dollars to start up companies that can come up with solutions in this space, notably Instagram, Pinterest, Tumblr, Snapchat, etc. The new platform Snapchat will allow postings that are not stored forever, so users between fifteen and forty years old are flocking to this platform away from Facebook.

WhatsApp Inc., has an application that lets users send free text messages for a whole year without paying anything. They have over 400 million users worldwide in a five year timeframe. This company

The Right Stuff Comes In Black

has recently been bought by Facebook for $19 billion. The new generation is flocking to this platform and traditional telephone companies actually lost $32 billion in revenues in 2014 because of the WhatsApp platform.

Smartphones allow access to the Internet and now mobile devices including tablets, e-book readers, laptops, are growing faster than personal computers. As my good friend Vint Cerf used to say when the internet was being developed at DARPA, no one imagined that the computer which is essentially the new smartphone will be moving from place to place in some ones pocket or carry-on bag.

News reporting has been equally transformed because if there is an earthquake like in Haiti, a person with a smartphone can take a picture and send it via the Internet for the news to travel around the globe before the traditional news media, print, or TV can report it. Eric Schmidt Chairman of Google recalled how a child in Haiti took a picture of her wounds during the earthquake and doctors were able to assess required treatment via the Internet.

Someone lost their camera while swimming on the beach in the United States and the camera found its way to Thailand. Someone else in Thailand discovered it, retrieved and developed the pictures five years later and placed them on Facebook. This allowed the owner of the pictures to be located in the United States. The global digital community/ village is here because of fiber optics and the Internet.

Telemedicine now allow doctors distance apart to review tele-radiographic data, mammograms, CAT scan data, dental records, and other data during surgery. As a matter of fact, remote surgical operations using robots have been carried out in war zones. This is because fiber optics and the internet allow transmission of enormous data, including real time video and pictures for the operation using the telemedicine platform.

These days, Skype video conferences and audio conferences (www.freeconferencecalls.com) are prevalent due to fiber optics. Join

The Right Stuff Comes In Black 32

Me (www.Joinme.com), a new application, can now permit two average online users to read documents displayed simultaneously on their respective computer screens even though they are thousands of miles apart. The author and his publisher used this technology to review and discuss parts of this book during the design stage. Fiber optics makes this possible.

Computer Games

At the moment the computer game consoles, like Xbox, are all interconnected to PC, mobile devices, and fiber optics to allow players distance apart to play together. Microsoft Xbox, electronic arts, and Japanese game makers like Sony are all expanding into this field. Microsoft Xbox is now incorporating features that will let seamless interaction with the connected home devices. Sony Play Station is also incorporating virtual reality features for the game experience.

E-Commerce and Online Shopping

Amazon which started as an online book store is now a major e-commerce giant selling electronics, computers, cameras, and many products. They were the first group to introduce the e-reader Kindle, with other competing e-readers like Nooks coming onto the market later. Fiber optics transmission allows digitized books to be distributed and sold online. Traditional bookstores, like Borders, could not compete, so they have been forced to shut down their brick and mortar stores. Barnes and Noble is implementing online book sales to survive. Traditional stores for clothing, shoes, are all implementing online shopping. The average shopper can browse online and do comparison shopping even before going to the mall. eBay has the online auction model where all products are sold; in fact Mark Cuban, who started the online music streaming Audionet before he sold it to Yahoo for $5.7 Billion, actually bought his forty-two million dollar private jet online.

The hospitality industries have a strong online presence where one can make reservation for hotels, rental cars, etc., anytime, anywhere on the mobile device.

The Right Stuff Comes In Black

All airlines have strong online ticket purchase program and have recently had to compete with Travelocity, Orbitz, and others. Fiber optics has enabled the Internet to become the place where with a few keystrokes, any customer can purchase all kinds of products or services online.

Dell Computer filled most of its computer orders online. This combination of online experience with brick and mortar shopping is creeping into the technology space. Apple Corporation is the first Silicon Valley company to have stores in malls and now Microsoft of Seattle has followed this transition.

So far the Internet sector has escaped sales tax in most states, but with the current protracted economic slump in the United States, most states are moving to impose tax on online shopping. The U.S. congress has also moved to enact legislation which will allow states to impose tax on e-commerce because they need new revenue to fund most state programs.

Impact on Education Through Online Teaching

Education can inspire generations as well as innovation and so Internet-based teaching and online courses are popular and proliferating around the world. In the United States, the nonprofit Coursera now has 2.5 million online students enrolled. Online education started two decades ago after the advent of fiber optics and the Internet. Coursera is using MOOCs (Massive open online courses) for this effort.

Coursera and MOOCs are leading this revolution with collaboration with many universities in the United States including Pen State, Stanford, MIT, and others. Tom Friedman, author of the book *The World is Flat* in a recent forum on online education stated that fiber optics connectivity and the Internet-based online courses provided by Coursera and MOOCs will enable people from all over the world to get higher quality education as provided by Ivy League schools in the United States, without setting foot in America. This is good because it is making higher education accessible to millions of students at lower cost all over the world.

Dr. Mensah's innovation in fiber optics technology and connectivity has impacted university education in ways unimagined thirty years ago, which is fueling the MOOCs revolution. Education in general is also being impacted by e-learning, through tablets and mobile devices like iPad and traditional personal computers; children as young as two years old can learn through games and interactive learning. Kiz.com is an example of this new platform that is enabled by fiber optics and the Internet.

The new K-12 digital platform for instruction in high schools recently launched by News Corp and Joe Klein of the New York school system, called *Amplify Tablets* is a game changer for e-learning and tablets for the classroom. The Amplify analytics and spot check will allow teachers to find out how students are absorbing material taught. The real time assessment tool is helpful to teachers. The five hundred billion dollar education market is ripe for competitive products like this. North Carolina has awarded a $500,000,000 contract to bring the system to the state. This platform also depends on the Internet and fiber optics.

Storage in the Cloud

In the financial arena, trillions of dollars are transmitted in few seconds routinely on stock exchanges around the world. The Cloud and fiber optics play a very strong role here because of the amount of data involved. In these days storage in the cloud is a huge business where virtual servers and mega severs hold secure data that can be accessed on demand when needed using fiber optics media transmission.

Amazon Web Services is valued at $2,300,000,000, growing faster than its traditional business with clients like the CIA, Netflix, and Lamborghini. This is a solely cloud-based business offering cloud storage to many businesses. In terms of data security in the cloud, the fiber optics media transmission itself is very secure; however, advanced software to support cyber security is facing daily challenges by computer hackers. The cyber criminals sometimes use phishing techniques to hijack financial account data, such as credit card information, etc., in this ongoing cyber war.

Most traditional publishing companies are getting into the digital world; Amazon was one of the leaders in creating its e-reader, the Kindle. We have already discussed Amazon's impact on the traditional bookstores.

Magazines are also getting into the digital act which is by far the most transformative effect since color of high quality was introduced to publishing. The mobile revolution is the new frontier where your favorite magazine will show up on your smartphone, tablet, e-reader, and laptop. All these digital transmission platforms are supported by fiber optics. This evolution is having an impact on the profitability of traditional newspapers which have increased their online presence. *Newsweek Magazine*, after several years of struggle, has now gone all digital to survive.

Big Data

The cloud has also spawned companies that store data on consumers, credit card information, Facebook photos, including personal information so that companies can tailor advertising according to one's preferences. The government also uses this data as well Internet companies. A new area that will see exponential growth is electronic health data and medical records. The connected home will also rely on big data as well as advanced sensors. The public has some reservations regarding Big Data especially when it comes to big government's access and use of such personal information.

This privacy issue is a big deal and will be debated for a long time since the average person does not want to be spied upon and would rather keep their private information and digital communications from the government.

The Right Stuff Comes In Black

In an experiment conducted recently, a small company was able to intercept and display cell phone calls in real time and display on a separate computer screen e-mails that were being transmitted by a third party. Cyber security and encryption are the solution against such intrusion on privacy.

Applications Include Internet Enabled Cell Phones

Fiber optics also allows smartphones and other mobile devices to retrieve data from the cloud where most of the computing is done. The command for search now can be voice or picture input (scanning a picture). The voice recognition algorithm can be used to translate information into different languages too. Combining heavy duty computation in the cloud with the minimal computing on the smartphone and transmission using fiber optics, voice commands can make life very interesting when one brings in the ability for translation to different languages. Tourism will benefit from this technology immensely. Google is one of the leaders in this field.

Movie Streaming

There is a trend now to do online streaming for movies, using TV set top boxes, and the cloud and fiber optics transmission play a strong role here too because of the enormous bandwidth of fiber optics. Many companies like Red Hut, Hulu, NetFlix, Verizon, Google, and Microsoft are all entering this online streaming market.

Hulu is projecting advertising revenues to grow from four billion currently to eight billion in a few years. Hulu Plus allows one to watch one thousand television shows on mobile devices, tablets, smartphones, etc., as well as traditional platforms, anytime. NetFlix inked a major deal recently with DreamWorks Studios that involved the purchase of several hours of content from DreamWorks.

Fiber optics transmission is the engine for movie streaming because of its enormous bandwidth. This would not have been possible with copper cables. The mobile web is the new frontier for online

The Right Stuff Comes In Black

advertising now and television networks are taking notice. ABC and others have created Internet applications which will allow the streaming of some shows online, as stated above.

The next challenge for all of us as leaders in the digital space when most consumers are adopting mobile phones, tablets, and laptops as a shift away from desktop and personal computers is *how to monetize mobile advertising*. This daunting challenge faces all Internet companies notably Google, Facebook, Yahoo, Twitter, Microsoft, and Dr. Mensah's Lightwave and Wireless Company.

The key innovation in this space is to display advertising on the small screens of smartphones. Dr. Mensah and his team are working on proprietary technology to meet this challenge.

He is also working with David Sheffer, a director of quality at Apple on some advanced products that cannot be described here.

Microsoft, mostly a software company, recently attempted to purchase Nokia, one of the largest global cell phone companies for billions of dollars, but could not reach agreement on the acquisition cost. This could be a game changer for Microsoft as it competes with Google. It was announced that Steve Ballmer, Microsoft chairman for decades, was leaving; and in less than a month after this announcement, Microsoft reached a deal to acquire Nokia for $7.2 billion. <u>To his credit, Steve Ballmer worked extremely hard to convince the Microsoft board to make this major acquisition.</u> The competition is on for new innovations in the handset arena. Samsung, Microsoft, Google, and Apple have to compete aggressively in this field. Microsoft now has the strength and the tools, including the Nokia acquisition, to forge ahead in this space.

Verizon Inc. has also made one of the largest acquisitions this year by buying the 45 percent stake in its joint venture with Vodafone, the German carrier, for $130 billion. This purchase allows Verizon Inc. to control 100 percent of the entity.

The Right Stuff Comes In Black

Google has already bought Motorola's cell phone division and deployed the Android platform and has even started laying fiber optic networks in selected cities for faster broadband transmission. Convergence of TV, computers, and voice communication is shown in the picture below and fiber optics make that possible and in a cost effective manner.

Barry Diller, the TV mogul, recently said in an interview on Bloomberg News that "in addition to online streaming of movies, content providers will seek to manage everything in the home, control of energy, remote video monitoring for security, etc. The convergence of telephony, computer data and television through the high bandwidth fiber optic cable transmission celebrated fifteen years ago is now here."

Home Entertainment

The new mobile tablets on the market are changing the way we watch television. One can watch Monday Night Football in the backyard. Apps from DirecTV can let the user watch live broadcasts and other contents. The user can also flick through a menu of movies or directly rewind accurately with the tip of the finger on the screen without the remote control. Direct streaming of content is only possible through fiber optics transmission.

Convergence of Video
Data Voice

The Broadband Internet

Sensor integration into all appliances in the home will help manage appliances as well as provide security for the home. Comcast Corporation and AT&T are big players in this field and recently Microsoft and others have entered this market. As discussed earlier in the wearable computing section of the book, the introduction of the smartwatch into the marketplace by Samsung, Sony, and Qualcomm, all based on the Android platform is a game changer. A smartwatch can also be used to control appliances in the home from the coffee machine to the air conditioner.

Electronic Payment System Using Cell Phones

The cell phone can be used to perform payment at the local grocery store, the mall, and other places. New sensors integrated into the smartphone will process payment from your checking account and perform other banking activities. The fingerprint sensor in the new Apple phone is important for security of the owner of the device, since the credit card information is involved for any mobile payment. Apple, Samsung, Square, and Microsoft are strong players in electronic payment using the smartphone. Jack Dorsey, founder of Twitter, has introduced Square an accessory to the smartphone for electronic payments; he is also interested in protecting users' PIN and other vital data. Twitter has also filed documents to do an IPO recently. This social media company has passed Facebook in advertising revenues on the mobile devices.

Dr. Mensah has also recently helped launch fiber optic based Internet radio in Atlanta. Internet radio is very popular and growing rapidly all over the world.

Cyber Security

Any connection to the internet must have safeguards with regards to cyber security, which as stated earlier is a software problem, because fiber optics transmission required for downloads from the cloud is very secure. Wi-Fi and the wireless connectivity require extensive encryption techniques regardless of location of use, such as

The Right Stuff Comes In Black

residential, business or public places, airports, stadiums, universities, etc.

Cyber security and encryption techniques are also important for the connected automobiles of the future. The video streaming in cars may distract drivers, and any cyber breach may even cause accidents.

The driverless cars as pioneered by Google Inc. may help even a blind person navigate the highways, however, there is more research required to make sure automated driverless cars may not experience safety issues arising out of computer malfunction or Internet hacking.

Safety in Flight: Boeing 787 Digital Sensors

The new Boeing 787 airplane has sensors on critical components that transmit airplane health monitoring data by satellite and fiber optics to the Seattle headquarters and operation center where engineers can monitor in real time these critical parts. This approach allows engineers to know what parts needs maintenance ahead of time. This is a new level of safety monitoring for aircraft while in operation around the world. Other global airplane manufacturers like Airbus may have to catch up on this next generation technology for insuring safety in the skies

Convergence of Television, Video, and Computer Data

Different Broadband Applications

The Right Stuff Comes In Black

Dr. Thomas Mensah was the invited speaker at the Columbia University's Seminar on Knowledge, Technology, and Social Systems, where he delivered a presentation on the topic: Impact of Fiber Optics: A Key Enabling Technology for the 21st Century.

Dr. Mensah in this presentation in New York also discussed next generation smartphones, cloud computing as well as the mobile transformation of the Internet.

Next Generation Internet

The next wave of innovation in Internet data transmission on optical glass fiber is based on Quantum Computing. Researchers funded by DARPA at University of Southern California led by Dr. Alan Willner and Boston University led by Dr. Siddharth Ramachandran [28] have proposed the use of a new laser beam, a donut-shaped laser beam called optical vortices as a replacement of current lasers. The team has developed a new optical fiber with an inner core surrounded by a concentric ring confined inside 8 micron diameter section with greater refractive index than the cladding. This fiber design allows two modes to propagate in the inner core and two modes in the concentric ring without mode coupling problems. The current lasers depend on Wavelength Division Multiplexing (WDM) to increase transmission bandwidth which has serious limitations. In this new optical fiber, lasers will not travel in straight path as 0s and 1s for data transmission but will travel along spatial modes within the glass fiber, each mode carrying several different colors or frequencies. The lasers will propagate in a helical manner along the transmission axis.

Optical Vorticles

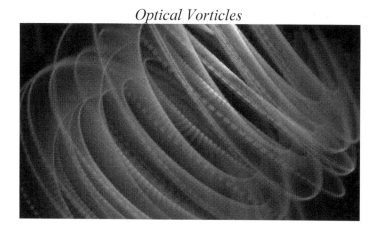

The new approach will solve the bandwidth limitation problem.

Allan Willner and his team developed the system that encodes and decodes the OAM pulses. The system encoded data into four separate channels. These four modes allowed transmission rates of 400 Gbits per second over 1.1 kilometer fiber.

OFS-Fitel company in Denmark and Researchers at Tel Aviv University were involved in the research [28]. Conventional manufacturing methods were used to make the fiber. The draw and coating process will use manufacturing techniques invented by Dr. Thomas Mensah to achieve lower manufacturing costs.

The implementation of this new fiber design will be confined to shorthaul and high density use in connecting virtual servers for cloud computing, not for submarine or longhaul applications because of the prohibitive cost involved.

Currently we transmit one thousand petabytes of data on the Internet every month. This includes photos, Youtube videos, emails, etc. And with current activity on social media, this transmission rate is increasing exponentially and could reach a limit unless we harness the optical vortices laser transmission technology. The total volume of all written data by human beings from the beginning to now in all languages is equivalent to 50 petabytes. Ten billion Facebook photos is 1.5 petabytes.

Dr. Mensah discussed these developments in a lecture at Georgia Institute of Technology, on the Future of the Internet at the recent American Institute of Aeronautics and Astronautics meeting on September 17, 2013.

Closing the Digital Divide

Dr. Thomas Mensah is interested in closing the "Digital Divide" in the United States and, overseas, especially in Africa. In the United States, Dr. Mensah is helping resolve this challenge through a contract he has with AT&T that is primed by Star Construction. This involves laying terrestrial fiber optic cable networks, including Internet broadband connection to cell towers. Mr. Bruce Clement, a vice president in Telecommunication Infrastructure deployment is one of the leaders in diversity in prime contracting in the United States. Dr. Thomas Mensah is doing this work through one of his companies, Lightwave and Wireless Corporation.

He is also concerned by low Internet connectivity in Africa, as demonstrated in the recent study by the Internet Society (ISOC.ORG) and is working to expand Broadband Internet into at least five countries in Sub-Saharan Africa. His company, Lightwave, has a partnership with GLORIAD, the Global Ring Advanced Network that connects supercomputers around the world. Dr. Greg Cole founded GLORIAD with initial funding from the National Science Foundation and this platform has grown to $200 million with support from companies like Tata Communication of India. GORIAD has connected Russia, China, Netherlands, Korea, and Japan.

Dr. Mensah is working with GLORIAD to upgrade broadband Internet using the ACE (Africa Coast to Europe), the Submarine Cable that reaches all the way to South Africa. Through the terrestrial network installation upgrade, Dr. Mensah is working on telemedicine platforms that will let doctors in Africa collaborate in surgery with doctors in America in real time as well as help train doctors in Africa through online teaching and e-learning. This will help doctors upgrade their certification and stay abreast of new developments in medicine. He has five doctors in the United States working with him on e-health and telemedicine platforms for this broadband Africa project led by Dr. Harold Jackson of Atlanta and Dr. Robert Bobby Satcher (former) U.S. astronaut at MD Anderson, Houston.

In Africa, his company Lightwave and Wireless Inc. has signed a Memorandum of Understanding with the Republic of Benin to upgrade their terrestrial broadband network, as well as enhance other infrastructures.

The Benin Ambassador to the United States Cyrille Oguin and the Ambassador to the United Nations Jean Francis Zinsou as well as Mr. Daniel Yohannes the CEO of the Millennium Challenge Corporation have been very helpful in this regard.

He has also met twice with His Excellency Dr. Thomas Boni Yayi, president of Benin, and immediate past chairman of the African Union on this program.

Dr. Mensah is also looking to expand broadband Internet networks in Ghana, Liberia, Democratic Republic of Congo (DRC), and Gabon. Dr. Mensah has also met with the Honorable Matata Mponyo, Premier of DRC, and Ambassador Dr. Faida Mitifu, who represents DRC in the United States. The President of DRC , His Excellency Joseph Kabila and his Cabinet are serious about modernizing key infrastructure in DRC. His proficiency in French has been helpful in these meetings.

In Ghana, His Excellency John Mahama and his ministers and staff, including the Honorable Mrs. Dzifa Aku Attivor for Transport, Mr. Samuel Sarpong, Central Regional Minister, Mrs. Mawuena Trebarh, Investment Promotions, Mr. Henry Adubofuor and His

The Right Stuff Comes In Black

Majesty Otumfuo Osei Tutu II, King of Ashanti are all serious about infrastructure development in Ghana.

In Liberia, Her Excellency Ellen Johnson-Sirleaf, the president, and the Senior Senator Jewel Taylor, as well as the Honorable Angelique Weeks, vice chairman of the Africa Coast to Europe, ACE Submarine Cable Consortium, led by France Telecom, and chairperson of the Liberia Telecommunication Authority, have been very helpful and supportive of infrastructure development in Liberia.

Dr. Mensah is also working on partnerships with major global entities for this undertaking because he believes that Africa is the next biggest market, after China and India, in broadband Internet use. This means that the upgrade of terrestrial networks with fiber optics and wireless network integration is key to bringing telecommunication and broadband Internet in Africa into the twenty-first century.

The recent trip by President Obama in June 2013 to the African continent, after his initial brief visit to Ghana, earlier on during his first term, indicates his willingness to deepen United States-Africa ties.

The United States is catching up since China has $200 billion investments in Africa compared to $100 billion by the United States. It is hoped that the United States can surpass China in the coming decades.

European countries and even Japan and Turkey are moving into African markets too.

Advanced Smart Munitions And Weapons

Dr. Thomas Mensah after receiving key patents in fiber optics manufacturing at Corning Inc. moved to AT&T Bell Laboratories. In the first year of this move he could not work in the manufacturing development area because of a certain clause in his previous contract at Corning Glass Works. AT&T decided to assign Dr. Thomas Mensah to a new project, the development of the first guidance system using fiber optics for smart missiles and munitions.

Just as he did at Corning Glass Works, in a short period of two years, Dr. Thomas Mensah and his team developed the first Fiber Optic Guided Missile system that allows smart missiles to hit targets.

In this technology the missile has a small camera in the nose cone that allows wide-angle pictures to be taken, digitized, and transmitted over the fiber while the missile is in flight. This allows the pilot in an airplane to lock on targets from a distance of six miles. Dr. Mensah received three patents on this technology including the Guided Vehicle Patent.

He and his team demonstrated missiles that traveled at speeds approaching Mach 1, the speed of sound. The crosshairs seen on television as missile hit target is a staple in our arsenal and Dr. Thomas Mensah and his team were the early innovators in this technology.

Smart missiles can now be directed through a window in a building without damaging other nearby structures.

Modern developments include GPS, laser-guided munitions that can be deployed on unmanned aerial vehicles, stealth aircraft, and other platforms.

Dr. Thomas Mensah and his company Georgia Aerospace currently works on technology for next generation cell phone batteries that can last three days without charging with materials created using the new field of nanotechnology.

The Right Stuff Comes In Black

THREE

Formative Years

Dr. Mensah was born in 1950 in Kumasi, Ghana, and attended Wesley College practice school in Kumasi. This high school had the best teachers, who came from teachers college and used the high school as training ground for future teachers. In 1963 he was accepted at one of the elite boys' school in Ghana—Adisadel College in Cape Coast. These schools, including Mfantsipim and another girls' school in Cape Coast, trained future leaders in medicine, science, engineering, and politics for the country. Kofi Annan, the past UN Secretary, attended one of such schools.

The picture displayed on the next page shows his dad, John Kofi Mensah, and his five boys. Tom is sitting in the front row on the far left. To his left is Osei Mensah, the youngest, now residing in Canada and Kojo Mensah on the far left. His senior brothers Samuel Owusu Mensah and Joseph Gyamfi Mensah are wearing Kente cloth like his dad in the back row.

The Right Stuff Comes In Black

A young Dr. Mensah is on the left side, front row

The Right Stuff Comes In Black

John Kofi Mensah was a successful business owner who owned cocoa plantations in Sunyani in the Brong Ahafo region in Ghana and a commodity store in Kumasi, the second largest city in this country. Tom's dad supplied cocoa to the chocolate factories in France. Tom was lucky to have his dad read to him at a young age; while sitting in his lap and at the tender age of four, he could read newspapers in English profusely.

His neighbor was a French teacher from Togo, a Francophone country to the east of Ghana, so by the age of eight, Tom spoke French fluently with French businessmen who visited his father's office for business meetings. Tom literally taught himself French by listening to the radio in French.

At Adisadel College his extracurricular activities included playing the violin, the clarinet, and finally the alto saxophone that won him a spot on the famous Adisadel Jazz Band. This band was exceptional and played for all the secondary schools in Ghana, and sometimes Tom served as a vocalist.

The picture below is from an article on a new effort to revive this jazz band. It shows the future fiber optics inventor as an eighteen-year-old young adult playing the alto saxophone. He is on the far right.

Young adult Dr. Thomas Mensah on the far right

The Right Stuff Comes In Black

Tom lived at Knight House dormitory throughout his college days at Adisadel, as he prepared for the O and A level exams. At this school, affectionately called Adisco, he excelled in Math and Science as well as French and actually won the French national competition in Ghana at both O and A levels.

On a typical Saturday at the end of the year, Tom would get up early to do drill with military corps, the equivalent of ROTC, and travel to Accra, the capital of Ghana to participate in the French competition. He would win first place prizes at Adisadel College in Math and other Science subjects, as well as French, in one busy day.

In his final year at Adisadel College he was elected a prefect in charge of booking events for the school. He dropped his musical stint after he finished O and A levels at the top of his class and was admitted to the Engineering school, Kwame Nkrumah University of Science and Technology (KNUST) in Kumasi. The list of those admitted was featured in the local newspaper.

In the Chemical Engineering Department he had great admiration for the intellect of Dr. Francis Aquah who taught Transport Phenomena and Unit Operations and Dr. Francis Allotey, first black to graduate in Physics at Princeton University, who taught Mathematics and Software Engineering.

Dr. Francis Aquah, who later became the Minister of Industry, was his first mentor. He was instrumental in introducing Tom to Chemical Engineering Research at the university level.

In 1974 Tom graduated at the top of his class with honors and won a French Government Fellowship to do graduate studies in Montpellier, France. The French government has been following his progress all along since winning the national competition. He was invited to take a special exam at the capital Accra that was to determine who will be the sole recipient of the French fellowship. He was requested to furnish a resume after he scored the highest point on the exam.

He received a prepaid plane ticket to France from the French government, settling in Paris initially, to get the appropriate instructions before heading to Montpellier in the south of France.

In Montpellier he stayed at the Cité Universitaire, a dorm for students close to the university. The fellowship paid for his tuition, lodging, books, and meals at the cafeteria and a small stipend so that he did not have to do part time work, but focus full time on his engineering studies.

In his first year he had to continue advanced studies in French because all the courses including advanced mathematics were taught in French. Some weekends, he joined other students from all over the world in the program as they toured various French castles, wineries, and cities in the Languedoc region.

Tom also took the DEA, the qualifying exams in Mathematics, Science and Engineering. He was then assigned to Dr. Henri Gibert, a leading Chemical Engineering professor from the Institute du Genie Chimique (IGC), the leading Chemical Engineering school in Toulouse, to work in his lab and be his graduate advisor. Professor Gibert taught some of the graduate engineering courses that Tom took at Montpellier University.

Tom visited IGC several times as part of his training, collaborating with other researchers and learning from leading engineers like Professor Pierre Couderc.

In 1977, Tom came to MIT with other top international students under MIT scholarship and received a certificate for a post graduate course in Chemical Engineering in Modeling and Simulation taught by MIT Professor Larry Evans of ASPEN fame.

Tom returned to France and completed his research graduating with honors in chemical engineering in 1978. Tom could count on Marie Christine, a fellow Montpellier student majoring in languages,

English and Spanish, as one of his best friends on campus during his college years in France.

His father visited him and his older brother Joseph who lived in London and convinced him to do further engineering research abroad rather than return to teach at KNUST in Ghana because of the political climate in the country. Dr. Thomas Mensah took his father's advice seriously and decided to move to the United States to further his career in late 1978.

Dr. Thomas Mensah migrated to the United States after his training in France where he settled initially in New Jersey in November of 1978. In the United States he maintained his connections at MIT and other engineering institutions, which he had developed during his studies in Europe, which will help him in his professional career.

One of his close friends, who he met at MIT, is Dr. Yaw Yeboah, who received four degrees from MIT in four years, including a PhD in Chemical Engineering and is now dean of Engineering at Florida State University. His other friend Dr. Richard Okine also received his PhD in Mechanical Engineering at MIT, now being a director at Dupont, while Dr. Isaiah Blankson, now a world leader in Hypersonics at NASA, received his PhD in Aeronautics from MIT.

All three like Dr. Mensah himself attended elite boys schools during their formative years. At one time MIT had one hundred top students from Ghana.

Dr. Mensah maintained his networks in other research institutions, which will help him later in his career.

The Right Stuff Comes In Black

FOUR

Fortune 500 Industry Experience

Air Products And Chemicals

Dr. Mensah was recruited to Air Products and Chemicals Inc. through his connections at MIT. At Air Products and Chemicals, his background in polymer materials processing was important for his first industrial project. He was assigned to solve a major industrial problem facing the Polyvinyl Alcohol Plant in Paducah, Kentucky. The plant process was interrupted frequently because of bottlenecks and problems associated with the high speed thin film mixers. After visiting the plant, Tom decided to develop and build prototypes to simulate the mixing process.

The mixing process involved a highly viscous non-Newtonian polymer, polyvinyl acetate (viscosity close to honey), and a catalyst of low viscosity of around one centipoise. Mixing occurs on the walls of these cylindrical mixers as the vertical blades move rapidly on the inner surface of the hollow cylindrical mixers and finally ejecting the mixed reacting polymer system onto a moving belt at the bottom of the hollow cylinder. The residence time was a few seconds. Dr. Mensah developed a simulator with transparent walls and prototype mixing blades with the same design configuration as in plant. He used a blue dye to represent the catalyst and observed that the mixing occurs primarily in front of the blades and the catalyst could not penetrate the complex Strauss secondary flow regime set up in front of the blades. He then created a moving blade system that traverses the surface of a flat plate and used a high speed video camera to capture the recirculating flows in front of the leading edge, as the blade moved mechanically across it. The non-Newtonian properties of the polymer led to the development of Strauss secondary flows that dominate the mixing process.

He designed notches in the blade to demonstrate that square notches were better than circular ones and the degree of mixing increased with blade speeds. He used these simulations to redesign the plant mixers and immediately resolved the plant stoppages with improved quality of the finished product. This was revolutionary work at that time.

He then submitted his findings to the Air Products worldwide symposium conference and won second place in the competition just after a year in the corporation. His findings were also published in the *Chemical Engineering Communication Journal* in 1984.

Corning Glass Works

In the early eighties, Corning Glass Works was experiencing significant problems as it transitioned fiber optics manufacturing to large scale production in its state of the art plant in Wilmington, North Carolina. It therefore put a search for a creative engineer to work at its main research center to help solve the problem.

In 1983, Dr. Mensah was offered this position as Senior Chemical Engineer Fiber Optics Development at the prestigious Sullivan Park-Corning Research Center in upstate New York. Sullivan Park is located on a hill and actually looks like an Ivory Tower where leading engineers, scientists, and innovators worked. The only difference was their frequent interaction with manufacturing facilities to help solve critical problems. Dr. Mensah was assigned to the fiber optics draw and coating process where the company was experiencing serious manufacturing problems. At Sullivan Park the atmosphere was of great camaraderie, where people interacted in a multidisciplinary manner. Frequently, the engineers would take the company plane to Wilmington to address manufacturing issues.

During one of these trips, the plant manager assembled all the engineering personnel into one place and told them that the plant would shut down, unless the glass fiber breakage problem was resolved. This problem was causing the plant to lose millions of dollars in operational costs. This threat was a strong motivator for serious collaboration amongst everyone involved.

Dr. Mensah had been working on this problem for a year and had come up with a solution at Sullivan Park. He had used high resolution video techniques to study the glass coating applicator problem and come up with a new design that he had patented. This was one of the shortest timeframes for a patent award to be implemented; six months since the patent application was filed, the plant wanted to use his invention.

Normally, to introduce a new design to a hundred million dollar plant requires years of test and study, but because of the pressure to resolve the problem, his invention was tested without delay on a dedicated draw tower. The impressive results were immediate, permitting fiber optics to be coated at higher speeds above the two meters per second for the first time without breakage or degradation in quality and performance. Speeds up to ten times the original speed were achieved with his design setting a world record.

Dr. Mensah received the Individual Outstanding Contributor Award and a check for $10,000 for this significant manufacturing innovation at Corning Glass Works. A schematic diagram and a picture of the process are shown on the next page.

Schematic Diagram of Fiber Optic Draw Process

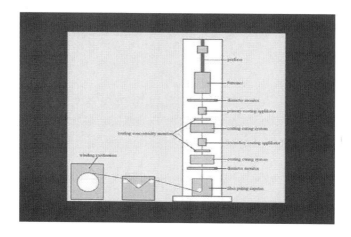

Photo of Draw and Coating Process

Fiber Optics Draw And Coating Process

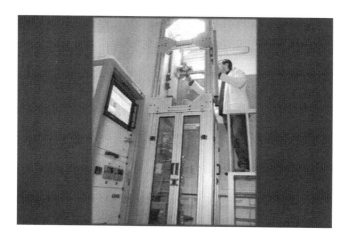

The Right Stuff Comes In Black

Elimination of Bubbles and Defects in Coated Optical Fiber

High speed fiber optic glass coating has unintended consequences because gases were entrained into the applicator that produced bubbles at the glass coating interface that led to light loses through microbend. This light loss affects computer and internet data transmission in fiber optics media.

Dr. Mensah used his understanding of boundary layer theory to design a system that involved introducing carbon dioxide gases at the entrance of the applicator leading to a novel process that eliminated gas entrapment problems.

He received a second patent for this invention, which allowed fiber optics to be produced at fifty meters a second with excellent optical fiber properties and high quality, setting another world record.

Dr. Mensah received two additional patents, one for the curing of optical fibers and the other for a system that permitted tension to be measured without touching the moving glass fiber, using a laser system and fast Fourier transform analysis. AT&T later used a similar approach after this invention and cited Dr. Mensah's patent.

One can control the entire draw process using the real time tension monitor, the fiber optics draw speed, the furnace temperature, and the preform feed rate as input parameters. The use of carbon dioxide gas produced defect-free optical fibers that are stronger and could be used for fiber optic-guided missile applications as well as for constructing submarine cables that connects different continents. This Innovation was important for extending the reach of the Internet platform globally.

AT&T Bell Laboratories

In 1985 at an optical fiber conference (OFC) in Atlanta, Dr. Mensah met some key researchers at AT&T Bell Laboratories. Dr. Mensah liked Atlanta and the warm weather in this Southern City.

The Right Stuff Comes In Black

AT&T Bell labs wanted to regain its competitive edge in large scale fiber optics manufacturing and had shown interest in the work done by Dr. Mensah at Corning.

In a short period of time after the Atlanta conference, Dr. Mensah received an offer to join AT&T Bell Laboratories. This research group like Sullivan Park at Corning Glass Works has international reputation; however Bell Laboratories was home to innovations beyond telecommunication. Vitamin B was invented here, so was the first satellite.

Nobel Prize winners in Physics like Arnold Penzias ran the AT&T Bell Laboratories. Dr. Mensah was thrilled to join this elite group of world renowned researchers at Bell Laboratories, following his breakthrough work at Corning Glass Works.

At AT&T, he could not work in the draw and coating area where he was the world leading expert for at least a year because of a certain clause in his contract at Corning Glass Works. Dr. Mensah was then assigned to a group tasked to develop a fiber optic-guided system for next generation missiles.

The Department of Defense in the past has relied on leading institutions like the RAND Corporation, the MIT Lincoln Labs, or AT&T Bell Laboratories to come up with revolutionary concepts and solutions for advanced weapons development.

The Fiber Optic-Guided Missile program involved winding ultra strong single-mode optical fibers on a mandrel about three inches in diameter and forming a stable package that can be inserted into the missile.

The optical fibers are connected to the electronics so that as the missile is launched it flies like an aircraft while a small camera in the nose cone gathers pictures of targets, digitize and transmit them over the unwinding fiber to the cockpit where they are displayed on the navigation panel as shown in the schematic diagram on the opposite page. The other pictures show missiles in flight and target engagement.

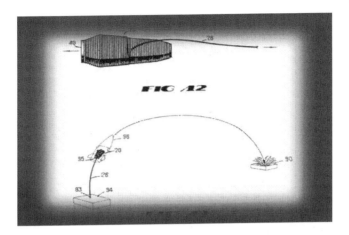

From Guided Vehicle Patent: Thomas Mensah

Smart Missile in Flight

Crosshairs for Smart Targeting

FOGM DISPENDING SYSTEM

This system allows the pilot to identify moving or stationary targets through target acquisition software, lock on them and affect a direct hit. For air to ground operations, moving targets like tanks can be tracked and hit accurately without collateral damage to civilians.

Dr. Mensah and his team developed an effective fiber optic-guided missile system that hit targets and met all the requirements of the stated mission. The team even tested a missile system with accurate targeting at speeds approaching the speed of sound (Mach 1). Dr. Mensah received three U.S. patents on the fiber optic-guided missile technology including the Guided Vehicle patent. Field testing at White Sands Missile Range, Eglin Air Force Base, and Redstone Arsenal were very successful.

Targeting Ships

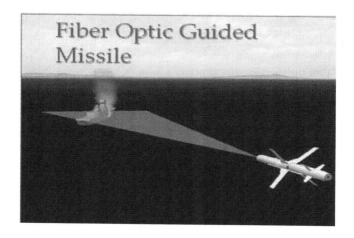

Launched Fiber Optic-Guided Missile

The Right Stuff Comes In Black

FIVE

Entrepreneurship

Working for three Fortune 500 corporations provided training and experience for Dr. Mensah to move into the entrepreneurial arena. The critical functions of business, notably technology, engineering, finance, accounting, manufacturing, HR, sales, and marketing can be easily learned in such corporate environments.

Supercond

Initially his innovation and primary work on advanced missile guidance technology development at AT&T Bell Laboratories led Dr. Mensah to form the high tech firm, Supercond Research Inc., to focus on advanced materials for the aerospace industry. He also had interest in the eight billion dollar Superconducting Supercollider project in Texas which caused him to travel to Texas several times to participate in this project. The name Supercond Technology came from this program. The United States was leading in this technology, however, after a few years, congress cancelled this project and the Europeans took the lead by implementing CERN, their competition to the Supercollider.

Dr. Mensah refocused his effort on advanced aerospace composite materials and in 1992 his firm was selected by the Department of Defense to work on a Mentor-Protégé program on the F-22, the stealth fighter being developed by Lockheed Martin Corporation. Dr. Mensah mastered all the processes and materials for

The Right Stuff Comes In Black

making components and advanced structures for this stealth fighter, the fastest supersonic jet in the world.

Even though emphasis has shifted these days from the F-22 to the F-35 stealth aircraft, the same technology is used in the manufacture of the new F-35 aircraft. This supersonic stealth fighter will be used by all armed services.

Dr. Mensah worked with Lockheed Martin Engineers and learned a lot from them because he already had a strong background in advanced composites technology and polymeric coatings and processing. He expanded his knowledge of autoclave processing of composites during this period.

After several years he decided to build and develop his own manufacturing plant to supply parts to defense contractors and the Department of Defense. Meanwhile he continued to collaborate with Oak Ridge National Labs, a DOE plant near Knoxville, Tennessee. He worked jointly with Dr. Steve Allison on a Department of Energy funded CRADA, awarded to him for him to work on integration of fiber optics into composite structures. He and Dr. Steve Allison successfully integrated flexible polymeric optical fibers into structures that have wide applications including smart bridges and weigh in motion systems and intelligent highways, as well as Advanced Aerospace Systems.

Georgia Aerospace Systems Manufacturing Inc.

In 2000, Dr. Mensah decided to expand into actual advanced manufacturing of aircraft parts instead of Aerospace R&D and so he kept Supercond as research division and founded a parent company, Georgia Aerospace Manufacturing Inc. He assembled a world-class management team of veterans in the aerospace environment, including Ken Cannestra, former President of Lockheed Martin Aeronautics, as well as his Defense Advisory Board members, Gen. Lester Lyles and Army Major General Jim Klugh and U.S. Marine

Corps Major Gen. Cornell West. He later brought on additional top leaders to guide him in this endeavor.

Dr. Mensah single handedly designed a state of the art aircraft composite manufacturing plant that was started up flawlessly, as shown in these pictures in North Georgia.

Georgia Aerospace won a major Department of Defense contract for advanced tactical platform development for the U.S. Air Force. His team worked with engineers in the Air Vehicle Branch of the Air Force, on the development of multiscale advanced composite structures for unmanned aerial vehicles.

Georgia Aerospace Manufacturing Plant

The plant has an Engineering Design Department, Manufacturing Department, Maintenance and Mechanical Department, Quality Control Department, Finance and Accounting, Final Product Testing, and Shipping Departments.

The headquarters of Georgia Aerospace is located in Atlanta so engineers and managers at the plant sometimes come to the headquarters for meetings. The executives at the headquarters frequently travel to the plant for some meetings.

Syspro Manufacturing Software was selected for the plant. This allows electronic manufacturing data to be also transmitted in real time to headquarters. This includes finance, production costs, and plant efficiencies for effective management.

Some of the advanced testing of composite parts produced at the plant was done at research centers around the country, like the University of Dayton Research Institute, under subcontract. This include ballistics test for structures, advanced thermal imaging for assessing performance of structures after ballistic impact, EMI tests, in-plane and through thickness thermal conductivity tests, etc.

Clean Room Processing of Composites

The actual hand lay up is done in clean rooms to produce defect free composite structures where humidity and temperature are tightly controlled. The positive pressures in the clean room help keep out particles that can reduce the strength of composites if found trapped in them. The lay up is done on tooling, composite or metal ones. For special applications like the stealth F-22 fighter jet, Invar tooling is used because of the excellent thermal coefficient of expansion properties.

Industrial Autoclave for Curing Composite Parts

EngineersOperating Autoclave

Autoclave Process Display on Computer Screen

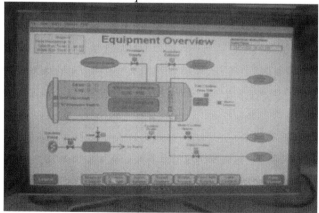

Computer Control of Industrial Autoclave

The Right Stuff Comes In Black

Novel Out of Autoclave Processing Technology

The new trend in composite manufacturing is "out of autoclave processing." This effort is to reduce manufacturing costs since autoclave processing is expensive. An aerospace autoclave can run from $300,000 for a decent size to over a million for large systems that can accommodate large structures like aircraft wings. The cost is also determined by pressure and temperature operating conditions.

Georgia Aerospace employs the Vacuum Assisted Resin Transfer Molding (VARTM) for out of autoclave processing and manufacturing of advanced composites. Processing occurs at lower pressures with enormous cost reduction. At the moment, secondary structures like those found inside the aircraft, including overhead bins, seat components, etc., can be produced with this process. The primary structures, like the leading edge of the stealth fighter, requires autoclave processing because of the high stresses involved in the aircraft as it travels at supersonic speeds.

Georgia Aerospace is currently a protégé of the Boeing Company, a world leader in advanced aircraft manufacturing and on lean manufacturing and the builder of the 787 Commercial Aircraft. The Boeing team and engineers are providing guidance and training in Lean processing of aerospace structures to Georgia Aerospace.

Vacuum Assisted Resin Infusion System (VARTM)

Engineers Assembling a VARTM for making composite parts

Digital Rapid Ply Cutters for
Composite Manufacturing

Georgia Aerospace has a very large and sophisticated rapid ply cutter on which carbon fiber both dry and prepreg are routinely cut for composite manufacturing as shown below. A large array of materials is cut with the computer controlled cutting machine. Vacuum system underneath the cutting table maintains the flatness of the sheet material during cutting operations. Other materials like Kevlar, fiber glass, film adhesives, thin plastics, and plastic vinyl are cut with the system.

The Right Stuff Comes In Black

Rapid Ply Digital Cutter

Georgia Aerospace Engineers working on the Digital Rapid Ply Cutter, DSC 2500. It is for cutting carbon fiber prepregs and Kevlar prepregs in the factory. The system is 10 ft. wide by 20 ft. long

Industrial Freezers

The carbon fiber prepregs and most raw materials are kept in industrial freezers at prescribed storage temperatures set by raw material suppliers like Cytec. These materials are removed to be cut on the rapid ply cutter when needed and unused materials sent back to the freezer for storage.

As mentioned earlier, Georgia Aerospace is a protégé of the largest airplane manufacturer in the world, the Boeing Company in a *Mentor-Protégé* relationship on Lean Manufacturing. The company has learned principles of lean manufacturing from the Boeing engineering team. Former Senator Sam Nunn of Georgia, previous chairman of the Senate Armed Services Committee established the Mentor-Protégé program through the U.S. Congress that pairs Prime Aerospace Defense contractors with businesses and aerospace second tier suppliers to the

Department of Defense. Georgia Aerospace is one of such companies which enjoy such special relationship with a mentor, the Boeing Company, the world's largest Aircraft Manufacturer.

The Right Stuff Comes In Black

SIX

Nanotechnology

Nanotechnology is the next revolution in Science and Engineering. Dr. Mensah is playing an active and significant role in this field. As a member of the Executive Committee for Nano Science and Engineering Forum in the American Institute of Chemical Engineers, he wants this forum to define industry and academic research in this field. He is the chief editor for a new book on Nanotechnology Commercialization process to be published by AIChE and Wiley Publications.

The field of nanotechnology involves manipulating at the molecular level carbon nanotubes so that their multifunctional properties can be used to enhance engineered products such as batteries, composite structures for aircraft, windmill blades, and other applications. The dimensions of carbon nanotubes are so small that scanning electron microscopes and tunneling electron microscopes are routinely used to study these materials. Dr. Mensah has established partnership with Florida State University, where one of the Nobel Prize winners for the discovery of carbon nanotubes, Dr. Harold W. Kroto, has an active research.

His company, Georgia Aerospace won a DOD contract in nanotechnology. Dr. Mensah served as the principal investigator on this program. He worked with the High Performance Materials Institute, where an innovative technique for dispersing and aligning single wall carbon nanotube using high energy superconducting magnetic field is being employed. The team developed techniques that allow real time observation of alignment of carbon nanotubes using a state of the art Raman Probe designed in this effort.

Dr. Ben Wang, former VP of Research, Florida State University, now director of manufacturing research at Georgia Institute of Technology; Dr. Kenwa Okloli, acting chair Department of Industrial Engineering; Dr. Richard Liang, director of HPMI, Florida State University; his colleagues at Eglin Air Force Base Mr. Lloyd Reshred, Branch Chief, and Lt. Aaron Doyle, program manager as well as Ms. Cathina Hill, Office of Small Business at Eglin Air Force Base all played an important role on this Air Force Project. He filed a provisional patent on a new process for nanotechnology sheets manufacturing in 2010 as part of this effort.

Dr. Mensah also collaborated with his friend Dr. Paul Ruffin, program manager at U.S. Army REDCOM in Huntsville, Alabama, on nanotechnology applications in next generation missiles, [21], and Dr. Joe Koo of University of Texas at Austin, on nanomaterials development for new thermal protective shields for rocket motors and space vehicles. [22]

Dr. Mensah has recently teamed up with NanoTech Labs in North Carolina, led by his friend Richard Czerf, to scale up a Carbon Nanotube sheet Manufacturing Process that produces up to 2–3 ft. wide and 200 ft. long CNT Sheets.

Georgia Aerospace has invested heavily in research in nanotechnology products at the company. The application of nanotechnology is extensive from batteries for cell phones, to solar cells, and windmill blades, leading to advanced products. Dr. Mensah believes that the United States can maintain its leadership in this field just like it did in the fiber optics revolution and Dr. Mensah and his team want to make sure that the United States continues to stay at the cutting edge of this development.

The Right Stuff Comes In Black

Advanced Batteries for Mobile Device

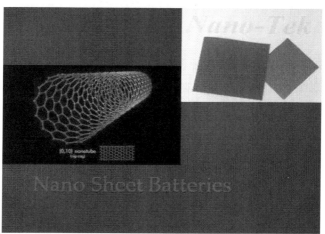

Nanotechnology Batteries for Cell Phones

*Nanotechnology Applications
Intelligent Smart Grid Technology*

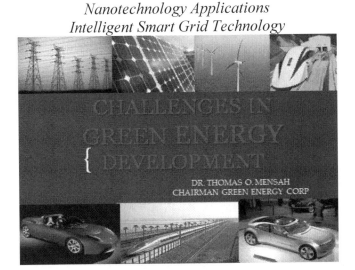

Various Applications from Solar Cells to the Smart Grid

Dr. Mensah and his team have successfully built and delivered to DOD two advanced composite structures for next generation Unmanned Aerial Vehicles Platforms.

He was selected to showcase results of some of his innovations at the 2010 National Nanotechnology Initiative (NNI) Conference at the Gaylord Hotel near Washington DC.

Some of his work was also presented and published at the AIAA Naval Weapons Effectiveness Conference Proceedings at the Naval War College in Monterey, California, in 2012.

Dr. Mensah cannot provide details of this effort in this book because it is classified by the Department of Defense and also involves some key proprietary data for Georgia Aerospace.

The Right Stuff Comes In Black

Historically Black Colleges and Universities

Dr. Mensah has signed a Memorandum of Understanding agreements with two historically black colleges and universities to establish nanotechnology centers, to train students and professors in this new area so that graduates will work in this new field that will generate most of the jobs in the coming decades.

Morehouse College in Atlanta and North Carolina A&T will serve as a model platform. Dr. John Silvanus Wilson, Morehouse's new president is working with Dr. Mensah to implement this program on Morehouse campus. Georgia Tech has a one hundred million dollar nanotechnology center on its campus. Morehouse will be the first HBCU to have a center like this in the nation,

Dr. Mensah intends to expand the number of institutions involved in these initiatives to ten. This will include Morgan State University (MD), Howard University, Jackson State University (MS), Bethune-Cookman University (FL), Prairie View A&M (TX), Spelman College in Atlanta (GA), Tuskegee University (AL), and University of Arkansas in Pine Bluff (AK).

Dr. Thomas Mensah is the chief editor of the book *Frontiers of Nanotechnology, Advanced Commercialization of Products, and Processes* in press by AIChE and Wiley Publishing Inc., NY.

Dr. Mensah's technology leadership in the United States has brought him into the company of major heads of corporations in the aerospace and defense industries, Internet companies, NASA, the U.S. military, heads of states, as well as other successful and famous individuals in movies, entertainment and politics. A few of these successful people are shown in the succeeding pages in the book.

The Right Stuff Comes In Black

Robert Stephens the former Chairman of Lockheed Martin Corp. and Dr. Mensah

The Right Stuff Comes In Black

Dr. Mensah with actress Vivica A. Fox.
Below: pictures with Thurbert E. Baker, Georgia State Attorney General

SEVEN

Recognition and Awards

Dr. Mensah has been recognized by several organizations, nationally and internationally. He was the invited keynote speaker at the United Nations Energy Forum in September 2009, and currently serves on the advisory board of the United Nations Energy Forum. He delivered a speech on green energy and nanotechnology implications on the Smart Grid Infrastructure in the United States.

In January 2009, Dr. Mensah was recognized by the Trumpet Awards Foundation, with the promenade of Distinction Award for his innovation in fiber optics. Ms. Xernona Clayton, president and executive director of the Trumpet Awards cited the pioneering work of Dr. Mensah that enable the average person to transmit pictures over the internet as well as send text messages via cell phones and handheld devices over long distances.

At the annual meeting of the American Institute of Chemical Engineers in Nashville, Tennessee., in November 2009, Dr. Mensah was named to the Executive Board of the Nano Scale Engineering Forum of the institute, the first and only black member of the board. He has been re-elected to serve another term on this Forum that shapes Nanotechnology Research directions in the United States.

The Right Stuff Comes In Black

Georgia Aerospace, his company was selected to showcase his innovations at the National Nanotechnology Innovations Initiative Summit in Washington DC in 2009.
His company was the only minority run firm at this showcase.

Dr. Mensah was also appointed to the U.S. High Speed Rail Organization Board.

At the Annual Meeting of Black Engineers of the Year Award (BEYA) in 2009, Dr. Mensah received recognition as Modern Day Technology Leader at the black-tie awards ceremonies in Baltimore.

In the same year Dr. Mensah was appointed to the NASA Space Consortium Board at Georgia Institute of Technology.

In 2008, during the centennial anniversary of the American Institute of Chemical Engineers, Dr. Mensah was named AIChE 100, an elite group of 100 Chemical Engineers of the Modern Era since World War II. This prestigious list of one hundred selected out of one thousand engineers in the United States include leading professors of Chemical Engineering, authors of leading textbooks in Chemical Engineering, innovators in industry, and presidents of universities. Top Ivy League institutions like MIT, Princeton, Cal Tech, etc., were included. Dr. Mensah was one of the only three blacks on this list of one hundred. See *Chemical Engineering Progress Magazine*, October 2008.

He has also received the Eminent Chemical Engineers Award from AIChE with Astronaut Dr. Mae Jemison in Philadelphia and participated on the MAC Eminent Engineers Forum that he helped established.

In 2007, Dr. Mensah received the Williams Grimes Award for Excellence in Chemical Engineering from the Minority Affairs Committee for his prowess in Chemical Engineering and mentoring young engineers in this field.

He was the invited speaker at the Columbia University for the Knowledge, Computers and Social Systems Program on which he spoke on the Impact of Fiber Optics a 21st Century platform on the Internet, mobile smartphones, and nanotechnology.

He was the invited speaker at UNESCO conference on Sustainable Development in New York last 2013.

Dr. Thomas Mensah is listed on Speakerpedia on "Internet and Technology" category alongside U.S. Astronaut Buzz Aldrin, the second man to walk on the moon; Dr. Peter Schultz, coinventor of fiber optics; Dr. Andy Grove, cofounder and retired chairman of Intel; Mark Zuckerberg, founder of Facebook; Larry Page, cofounder of Google; Jack Dorsey, founder of Twitter; Bill Gates, cofounder of Microsoft; Dr. L. Rafael Reif, president of MIT, and other technology innovators.

EIGHT

Service to Professional Societies in the United States

Dr. Mensah was appointed to the Board of Trustees of the AIChE Foundation in 2009.

Dr. Mensah was appointed to serve on the MIT visiting committee/ Industry Advisory Board from 1988 to 1992. This group advises the MIT Corporation on advances in engineering.

Dr. Mensah was elected to the Governing Board of Directors of the American Institute of Chemical Engineers where he served from 1987–1990.

In 1987, Dr. Mensah was elected as the national chairman of the Materials Engineering and Sciences Division of AIChE, the first black to hold this position. Dr. Mensah expanded programming to include new areas like electronics, ceramics, fiber optics, etc., which has led to other new areas like MEMS and nanotechnology.

Dr. Mensah organized and chaired several sessions at annual national meetings in fiber optics, superconductors, etc., and served as editor of two symposium book volumes in these cutting edge subjects, which are sold on Amazon and featured in engineering libraries around the world.

The Right Stuff Comes In Black

In 1985, Dr. Mensah was elected and served as chairman of the Twin Tiers section in New York. (*Chemical Engineering Progress Magazine* 1985)

He was one of the first chemical engineers to propose that the National Organization refocus its activities and expand them into green and renewable energies. This has been done and sessions are now organized in these areas.

As director on the Nanoscale Engineering Forum he has organized and chaired session in nanotechnology implications on the Smart Grid infrastructure and renewable energy, including novel polymer solar cells.

Dr. Mensah is also playing an active role in another engineering society, the American Institute of Aeronautics and Astronautics (AIAA).

He was elected and served as the first and only black chairman of the Atlanta chapter and is now Deputy Director of Technology for Region II in AIAA.

He was recently elected to Associate Fellow Level in AIAA at the Nashville AIAA Annual Sciences meeting. He is one of the few blacks in the world to hold these titles in two prestigious engineering organizations, Chemical and Aeronautics in the United States.

Dr. Thomas Mensah also won the Percy Julian Award, which is named after the famous African American inventor, who had to go to Germany to obtain his doctorate because major Ivy League institutions in his days would not admit a man of color. He graduated returned to the United States and made major contributions in Science, including the discovery of cortisone, the well-known drug for arthritis, and invented the foam used by the U.S. Navy. Percy Julian was subject of a highly publicized PBS Documentary, "The Forgotten Genius."

JIMMY CARTER

December 6, 2002

To Thomas Mensah

It is a great honor to be awarded the Nobel Peace Prize, particularly as The Carter Center celebrates its 20th anniversary. Rosalynn and I deeply appreciate this affirmation of the importance and effectiveness of the Center's mission to wage peace, fight disease, and build hope around the world.

Our work and this international recognition are only possible because of the partners we are blessed to have. Because of your encouragement and support, millions of people have better lives and hope for their families. In a very real sense, you share the Nobel Peace Prize with us. We thank you for your friendship and believing in our work.

Sincerely,

Jimmy Carter

Dr. Thomas Mensah
President and CEO
Georgia Aerospace Corp
75 Piedmont Avenue NE Suite 3
Atlanta, GA 30303

Top: Former President George W. Bush and Dr. Thomas Mensah in Georgia

Bottom: Actor Morgan Freeman and Dr. Mensah discussing online movie streaming

Top: Secretary of State Hilary Clinton and Dr. Mensah in Washington DC

Bottom: Former Governor of Georgia Sonny Purdue in Atlanta

Top: Dr. Mensah with U.S. Senator Johnny Isakson in Georgia

Bottom: With General Lester Lyles, former Materiel Commander of U.S. Air force (retired)

Top: Former Senate Majority Leader Bill Frist and Dr. Mensah in Atlanta

Bottom: With Dennis Hastert 59th Speaker of the U.S. House of Representatives

The Right Stuff Comes In Black

Top: With Blue Angels Pilot Donnie Cochran and another U.S. Naval Officer

Bottom: With Former Secretary of State Condoleezza Rice now at Stanford

The Right Stuff Comes In Black

Top: With Former U.S. President Bill Clinton

Bottom: With Actress, Producer Debbie Allen discussing Success Park in Atlanta

The Right Stuff Comes In Black

Top: With General Colin Powell, former Chair of the Joint Chiefs and former cabinet Secretary of State, in Washington DC

Bottom: Dr. Thomas Mensah with Actor Chris Tucker in Atlanta at the Trumpet Awards Ceremonies

Top: BET Founder and TV Mogul Robert Johnson and Dr. Mensah in Washington

Bottom: Dr. Mensah with Art Carter former Vice President Boeing Missiles Group

Top: Dr. Mensah with Senator Carl Levin, Chairman of Senate Armed Services Committee

Bottom: Dr. Mensah with the 44th U.S. President Barack Obama in Washington DC

Top: Dr. Mensah with former UN Ambassador Andrew Young in Atlanta

Bottom: With Rep. Sanford Bishop, Mayor Shirley Franklin, and Rep Gregory Meeks

Top: With Rep. Bennie Thompson, Ranking Member Homeland Security Committee in the House

Bottom: Dr. Mensah with Marc Morial, Current President, National Urban League

Dr. Thomas Mensah
75 Piedmont Avenue, NE,
Suite 340
Atlanta, GA 30303

Dear Friend,

I would like to thank you most warmly for your kind words on the award of the 100th Nobel Peace Prize.

The prize is truly an honour for the whole United Nations — its Member States and our dedicated staff around the world. The award also reflects the essential contribution of individuals worldwide, in government, business, academia, the media, and civil society in all its forms, who do so much to promote the United Nations, its work, and the principle of international cooperation. Above all, the Prize is a tribute to our colleagues who have made the supreme sacrifice in the service of humanity.

At this time of global uncertainty, the UN faces both increased challenges and new opportunities. Your expression of support at this time comes as a source of encouragement and inspiration to me personally, and to all of us who work in the Organization. With your help we will succeed in building peace and better lives for people all over the world.

Congratulatory letter from former United Nations General Secretary, Kofi Annan, currently Chairman of Agriculture Development in Africa and a personal friend.

The Right Stuff Comes In Black

Top: Dr. Mensah with Saxby Chambliss, U.S. Senior Senator from Georgia

Bottom: Dr. Mensah and Dr. Kase Lawal Chairman of CAMAC Corporation at AIChE Awards Program

Dr. Mae Jemison, first black female U.S. Astronaut, and Dr. Thomas Mensah, recipients of the Eminent Engineers Award.

The Hon. Lisa Jackson, Vice President at Apple Corporation with Dr. Thomas Mensah, Eminent Engineer Awards 2013

Dr. John Sylvanus Wilson Jr, Morehouse President And Dr. Thomas Mensah

Mrs. Xernona Clayton Founder and CEO of the Trumpet Awards Foundation with Dr. Thomas Mensah at Trumpet Awards

Dr. Thomas Mensah with NASA Administrator Charles Bolden in DC

**AT&T Fiber Optic Cable Ready For Installation
For Internet and Advanced Telecommunication Networks**

The Right Stuff Comes In Black

NINE

Green Energy Revolution

Dr. Mensah had a few ideas when our national leaders were looking for answers to help *solve* the U.S. economic crisis. He felt strongly that the stimulus package that was being designed in 2009 should have a very strong infrastructure component. Having been a key player in the broadband and fiber optics infrastructure deployment, he felt he should communicate his ideas to the leaders of our country.

He spent time to develop a white paper entitled "Twenty First Century Advanced Transportation System for America." In this paper Dr. Mensah provided the intellectual argument for high speed rail development and deployment in the United States. He wrote a letter first to Warren Buffet, a Wall Street business icon and sent a copy of his white paper to him. He also wrote a letter to the President of the United States and sent a copy of his white paper in which he strongly recommended that the United States should look at high speed rail, particularly steel on steel not the MAGLEV because of the cost per mile efficiencies. Mr. Buffet has recently purchased Burlington Northern for over $1 billion and therefore has become a rail operator, a growth area in the U.S. economy.

Dr. Mensah was one of the early and first proponents of high speed rail as a means of reducing carbon footprint and creating jobs.

The Right Stuff Comes In Black

When President Obama was elected as President of the United States, Dr. Mensah had a letter sent the day after his inaugural, on the twenty-first of January 2009. Copies of the letter were sent to key senators and members of Congress, the Secretary of Transportation as well as the Vice President of the United States.

Dr. Mensah was pleasantly surprised that most of his recommendations in the white paper have been adopted by the administration and was glad to see the President announce on CNN America's high speed rail development initiative in the country. He received a letter from the Vice President of the United States who is in charge of the Economic Recovery Act thanking him for helping the administration shape their agenda.

The white paper that Dr. Mensah wrote had some novel concepts touching on Advanced Battery development for electric cars, to advanced luggage tracking systems on trains so it will not be reproduced here for wide public dissemination. Dr. Mensah has been appointed to the U.S. High Speed Rail Organization Board in Washington DC. Dr. Mensah was also a keynote speaker at the United Nations Energy Forum in 2009.

The High Speed Rail in the United States became a political football, with some governors sending the initial investments back to Washington. This could have produced significant jobs in those states in this era of prolonged high unemployment. Only California and the Midwestern states have pushed High Speed Rail. A strong job component is necessary for dealing with the economic and debt crises in America.

Manufacturing jobs from the High Speed Rail could have made up for those jobs lost to other countries especially China and India. Now America has to wait for the recovery in the housing sector, even though people with jobs can help this sector recover faster because they can take on mortgages and buy homes.

Infrastructure Development should not be a political issue, anything that creates manufacturing jobs in this country will help

America deal with this prolonged unemployment and economic crisis. The recent unanimous Senate confirmation of former mayor Anthony Foxx as U.S. Transportation Secretary hopefully will generate some enthusiasm and support for this important infrastructure project for the United States to catch up with Japan, France, Germany, Spain, and China.

The Chinese on the other hand have leapfrogged America in High Speed Rail development, and now have over forty High Speed Rail lines, even though at the time when Dr. Mensah made his recommendations to the White House, they had only two.

China is moving goods and people faster and making serious economic progress. China is growing at three times the rate of growth in western countries like the United States. They now provide loans to America and many countries. They have at least a billion people to feed so their focus is on infrastructure development and investments. Their economy continues to grow as they systematically embrace and adopt western concepts, including our major innovations in research, our aircraft technology, manufacturing technology, business expansion strategies, and infrastructure developments. Most U.S. computer and high tech companies like Apple Inc., as well as large distribution companies like Target and Walmart do their manufacturing in China providing jobs there. China may have serious human rights problems, but they want to compete with the United States in manufacturing and technology.

The Right Stuff Comes In Black

TEN

Creating The World Success Park, Including The First African American and Latino Theme Parks

For the past ten years Dr. Mensah has been developing by far one of his most imaginative and inspirational projects that draws on his vision, talent, and creativity. The conception, creation and development of the *World Success Park*, an amusement theme park that will showcase the success of all races in the world. Different sections of the park focus on different races and their heritage—from American Indian Tribes, to blacks, Latinos, Asians, Europeans, and people from the Middle East. Success Park China, for example will showcase the success and culture in China. Latino Success Park will showcase Hispanic Heritage including the incredible achievement of my good friend US Astronaut Franklin Ramone Chan-Diaz who traveled into Space 7 times and was recently inducted into the Space Hall of Fame in 2014 with Astronaut and Senator John Glenn. Success Park Japan, will showcase the Japanese culture, and so forth.

The first African American amusement/theme park in the world will showcase black heritage and success. He calls this theme park

The Right Stuff Comes In Black

Success Park USA. This is Dr. Mensah's answer to a Black Disney World. Dr. Mensah has applied for and received a U.S. Patent Office Trademark on this park (see figure below). Like most of his inventions, Dr. Mensah set out to solve an important challenge and dilemma facing people of color, African Americans and blacks throughout the world, the lack of common identity and connection to their roots. Italian Americans have connection to Italy, Chinese Americans have connections to China, French Americans to France, and so forth. He looked at this challenge in the same way scientists and physicists have tried to develop the Unified Theory.

Dr. Mensah has been working day and night to develop this theme park. He envisions a park in which blacks do their DNA test and after finding their country of origin or roots on the continent like Alex Haley did, can go to a place in the park that represents their country and be treated like a long lost kin, as in the biblical Joseph story, and be exposed to the culture, music, and food while wearing the traditional clothes—right here in the USA. The psychological impact on black children will be far reaching and incalculable, finally bringing them connection to their ancestry.

Dr. Mensah has created versions of this park for Latinos to be built on the West Coast, and eventually, a World Success Park where the success of all races will be represented. He has applied for patents on these innovations.

This park was first announced in *Ebony Magazine* in October 2006, during an interview and a profile on blacks in Technology. Incidentally a month after this announcement, the Disney Corporation announced that it will create its first black princess movie, which has been done recently. The black princess made $25 million for Disney in just one weekend. This is progress for all of us. Dr. Mensah wants the park buildings in his Success Park to be environmentally friendly and LEEDS certified as much as possible economically. The park will be the first environmentally friendly theme park in the world. Dr. Mensah has discussed the Success Park China with two governors from China who are very interested in locating the park in their provinces.

He intends to locate the first park, Black Success Park, in Georgia, not far from Atlanta. The park will have streets named after black heroes namely Nelson Mandela Highway, Dr. Martin Luther King Jr. Circle, Rosa Parks Highway, Bishop Tutu Way, Arthur Ashe Street, Muhammad Ali Boulevard, Bob Marley Street, Kwame Nkrumah Boulevard, Kenyatta Highway, W.E.B Du Bois Highway, Elijah Muhammad Boulevard, etc. The park will feature pyramids with restaurants in them, and children will ride in miniature Egyptian chariots to remind them of their connection to Africa.

World Success Park: Dr. Mensah's Vision

Patent pending USPTO [Mensah Inventor]

The Right Stuff Comes In Black

Grand Opening of Success Park USA
(A Movie and TV Experience)

For the first African American amusement park, Dr. Mensah will also reflect on *black* success from two hundred years ago, when slaves travelled from the continent of Africa to the continent of North and South America till now.

Another interesting vision of his is to also redo the Middle Passage, twenty-first century style. He intends to organize a special Middle Passage voyage and experience, starting from the slave castles in Africa like Ghana, Angola, Gore Island, and traversing the Atlantic Ocean, retracing the paths that our ancestors took on their voyage to America. This journey will be used to promote the grand opening of the park. This time he wants blacks to be transported in a nice ship, no chains, but all occupants of the ship will be dressed in fine linen, preferably white. This is a voyage of celebration and triumph over adversity that happened two centuries ago. When they reach locations, that historically speaking, blacks who were too sick to make the journey because of the conditions of travel, *were tossed overboard into the ocean*, the ship will slowdown for proper burial rights and prayers to be performed by their great-great-grandchildren who live today in the United States, Brazil, and the Diaspora.

As the occupants of the luxury ship traverse the seas, their ancestors will look down from heaven, saying we came in chains under horrible conditions in a slave ship, but our children are making this voyage heading toward *Success Park USA* in fine clothes, drinking champagne, and celebrating the triumph of the human spirit. It is appropriate that they have not forgotten those who died during the trip when they were transported on slave ships.

An important event that will occur on this cruise is the engagement of the Millennium, where two couples fall in love on the cruise and get engaged. Two Ceremonies will be performed one according to the traditions of the motherland followed by the usual

The Right Stuff Comes In Black

engagement ceremony as we see in the United States. The actual wedding called the wedding of the Millennium will occur at the First African American Theme Park in the US, when the Cruise Ship lands on the East Coast of America. During Slavery each passenger could not marry but were sold as soon as the ship lands in America. The Movie can be called the Wedding of the Millenium or the wedding of the Century.

Upon arrival on the East Coast of America, huge gatherings of both blacks and whites will welcome them in Savannah, Miami, Charleston, Brunswick, near former slave markets, but this time they will hug them and welcome them as they did on Ellis Island, not to be sold as before. This time they will board luxury busses that will transport them to Success Park USA. In the park they will be joined by living legends of the Black race including Muhammad Ali and all other great icons of the Black Experience.

In the park they can experience technology at its best as it relates to the development of the slave ship simulator in which Dr. Mensah brings history and activities that occurred two hundred years ago to the twenty-first century for today's children to learn and experience history, using virtual reality.

This Mid Passage cruise will be filmed for TV viewing; a movie version will be produced and distributed worldwide in movie theaters and cinemas.

Dr. Mensah is in negotiations with TV and Movie producers in Hollywood for this innovation in the Black Experience. He has discussed this project with Quincy Jones, Lionel Richie, Robert Brown (B&C North Carolina), and brief details of the Success Park with Oprah Winfrey, Debbie Allen, and Magic Johnson.

He intends to discuss the Latino Success Park Development with leaders in the Latino community in Los Angeles including the former Mayor Antonio Villaraigosa, actress Salma Hayek, and entertainer George Lopez on the *West Coast and other Latino leaders in Miami, and Texas.*

The Right Stuff Comes In Black

ELEVEN

Recognition

Dr. Mensah has been nominated for induction into the Internet Hall of Fame created by the Internet Society, headquartered in the United States (www.internetsociety.org). He was nominated for his pioneering contributions and innovations in Fiber Optics by bringing the cost of Fiber Optics to the same level as copper media, leading to the replacement of copper by this more efficient transmission media. His innovations led to high strength defect-free optical fibers used specifically for submarine applications extending the global reach of internet to other countries and continents.

As a chemical engineer, Dr. Thomas Mensah was named one of the 100 Modern Engineers at the centennial celebration of the American Institute of Chemical Engineers; this is a list of one hundred innovators selected out of one thousand engineers throughout the United States. He is one of the youngest and one of three blacks on this list. This list included professors and renowned educators in chemical engineering, university presidents of Ivy League schools, and experts and pioneers in Industry.

Dr. Thomas Mensah has won the Promenade of Distinction award by the Trumpet Awards foundation established originally by Mr.

Ted Turner and Mrs. Xernona Clayton the founder that recognizes African American achievers. Other awards include Golden Torch Award, the highest award by NSBE, the Society of Black Engineers in the United States, the Williams Grimes Award of Excellence in Chemical Engineering, and the Eminent Chemical Engineers award by the Minority Affairs Committee of the American Institute of Chemical Engineers.

Dr. Mensah was recognized in 2012 with the Diamond Award for his innovation in Aerospace and Fiber Optics at a Black Tie Gala at the Ray Charles Performance Center at Morehouse College in Atlanta, where he revealed the details of his World Success Park project publicly for the first time. He has supported the Trumpet Awards and the Not Alone Foundation (Diamond Awards) in the past few years.

Dr. Mensah was Elected Associate Fellow of another prestigious engineering society. The American Institute of Aeronautics and Astronautics, whose past members and fellows include Von Braun, founder of the U.S. Rocket and Space Program, and the Wright Brothers who invented the airplane.

Dr. Thomas Mensah has been named in 2014, as the Chairman of the Scientific Council of the United Nations Energy Forum. This Forum has a mission to insure that Developing and Emerging Countries have access to Energy and Cheaper Electricity for Industrialization. These National and International recognition of Dr. Mensah is important in the light of the fact that blacks are not well represented in Technology.

A recent article in USA Today Weekend Edition, June 1 2014, shows that the work force distribution at Google Inc. in Silicon Valley; is 60% White, 30% Asian, 3 % Hispanics and only 1% Black. This situation must be addressed, since the 30 Million Blacks in this country also use the Google Search Engine. I think in fairness Blacks should also look at other options like the Bing Search Engine from Microsoft, since at least Microsoft has appointed John Thompson an African American who served on the Board as Chairman of Microsoft in 2014.

The Right Stuff Comes In Black

TWELVE

Technology Development on the Continent of Africa

Dr. Thomas Mensah also spends part of his time on Technology Transfer that will help bring Africa into the twenty-first century, beginning with plants that will generate 30 MW of electricity in a few select countries, building fiber optic networks for Internet and telemedicine applications in Africa. His fiber optic company Lightwave and Wireless Inc., which currently has contracts to connect cell towers with fiber optic cable for AT&T through Star Construction, is leading the fiber optic installation in Africa. Mr. Bruce Clement, a vice president is a strong leader in promoting diversity in Fiber Optics programs at majority firms in the United States.

Dr. Mensah's green energy company has a joint venture with Inviron and Green Power Company of Florida to develop electricity-generating plants in Africa. This company is led by his colleague Dr. Neil Williams, inventor of the plastic liners for landfills and a world expert in gasification of solid waste. He has other businesses that are in the infrastructure construction, as well as healthcare and telemedicine which are going. He is taking U.S. investors and developers that will build modern airports on the continent and also provide electricity to a select few countries.

He is very excited that Kofi Annan is focusing on Africa after several years at the head of the U.N., with a partnership with Richard Bronson. Bono, the lead singer of the U2 band is focusing on Africa, as well as Bill and Melinda Gates Foundation in the health sector. His good friend Bob Johnson, founder of BET, is already in Liberia with a large hotel on the beach in West Africa.

As CNN pointed out, Africa will be the third largest market after China and India, so he believes the United States should pay close attention to this continent instead of allowing China to dominate developments on the continent.

We need engineers and businesses that can build things in Africa. The current new advanced countries like Israel, China, Malaysia, and Korea relied on its citizens trained abroad and living in places like the United States to connect with executives and managers in these countries and together accomplished Technology Transfer and Investments to their respective countries. This team approach can solve the problems of poverty, diseases, unemployment, and help stabilize political institutions on the continent. He feels with all his training and successes in cutting-edge technologies and innovation demonstrated in the United States and elsewhere, he at least owes that much to the people of Africa and the continent where he spent his formative years.

Dr. Thomas Mensah with His Excellency Dr. Boni Thomas Yayi, President of the Republic of Benin and Mr. Daniel Yohannes, CEO of Millenium Challenge Corporation Benin Economic and Investment Forum, Waldorf Astoria, New York City.

United States Energy Assistance to Africa

President Obama has pledged $7 billion to support Electricity Development in countries in Sub-Saharan Africa, during his June 2013 trip to the continent. According to the President, without "Electricity" vaccines cannot be refrigerated in storage, healthcare suffers, factories cannot open to provide jobs and economic development, computers will not work, children cannot study at night and real development is not possible. Africa is poised to become the next major world market with its one billion population that will double by 2050.

This huge market cannot be penetrated if electricity is not made available in the different countries. Africa grew 6 percent in GDP this year while most Western nations grew at 3 percent; helping the continent solve its energy problem is the key to creating this huge market. This could be President Obama's signature achievement, similar to what President George Bush did for Africa on the Aids prevention assistance, Dr. Mensah wants his Renewal Energy Program that transforms solid waste to Electricity using Gasification Technology for countries like Ghana, Liberia, Benin, DRC, and Gabon to be a key part of this United States initiative since the president is a strong advocate for reducing the global carbon footprint in this decade.

During the Africa Summit held from June 6 through 8, 2014 in Washington DC, Dr. Mensah presented copies of his book to, His Excellency Boni Thomas Yayi, President of the Republic of Benin, His Excellency Joseph Kabila President of the Democratic Republic of Congo, and His Excellency Teodoro Obiang Mbasogo, President of Equatorial Guinea. The Summit organized by the US President, President Obama, raised $38,000,000,000 in Private Capital to help infrastructure development in Africa.

The Africa Leader's summit was attended by 47 African Heads of State from Africa as well as major American Companies and Business leaders including Mayor Michael Bloomberg, Chairman of the Bloomberg Foundation. This Summit was very successful and addressed several topics including Security, Health, US Investments in Infrastructure and Good Governance. Dr. Thomas Mensah attended and participated in the Summit.

OFFICE OF THE VICE PRESIDENT
WASHINGTON

August 25, 2009

Thomas Mensah
P.O. Box 54737
Atlanta, GA 30308

Dear Thomas:

Thank you for sharing your thoughts and taking the time to write me.

This is an extraordinary moment in our nation's history and having the benefit of your views is helpful in shaping our Administration's agenda.

Again, thank you for sharing your thoughts and I encourage you to stay engaged and interested in your government.

Sincerely,

Joseph R. Biden, Jr.

The Right Stuff Comes In Black

THIRTEEN

The Power of Faith in God in His Life

Dr. Thomas Mensah credits strong faith in God for his great achievements and success in life—from humble beginnings at Adisadel College days, to KNUST, Montpellier University, and MIT and working on projects at world leading research institutions and for the Department of Defense-Pentagon in the United States.

His work in industry, air products, and world renowned prestigious scientific labs such as Sullivan Park at Corning Inc. and AT&T Bell Laboratories, prior to founding Georgia Aerospace Corporation, Lightwave and Wireless Corporation and other entrepreneurial endeavors.

He meditates daily on scriptures, and has seen God work in all areas of his life. Dr. Mensah has been invited speaker not only to engineering and scientific organizations, the United Nations, major universities and other nonprofit groups but also to church organizations. He has relied on God as the source for wisdom, creativity, tenacity, focus, and strength for all his successful endeavors. He prays constantly and fast regularly. Dr. Mensah can recount many instances that God has intervened miraculously in his life, starting from his childhood as a baby when he was thrown out of a car after an accident, in which all occupants in the vehicle were hurt including his mother who held him in her lap as he slept; and at the hospital, she inquired where was her baby, after regaining consciousness and was told that her baby was safe without any scratches. He credits God for sending angels to hold him safe in the air and protecting him from that accident.

He also recalls an incident recently which reminds him of the account of Shadrach, Meshach, and Abednego in the old testament scriptures, who were thrown into a fiery furnace for refusing to bow down and worship any human other than the True Almighty God. This story is recounted in detail in the Holy Scriptures and will not be repeated here. Dr. Mensah was cooking and forgot that he had left food in a pot on the stove. He had stopped to visit some friends about a mile away. The kitchen and the entire place were filled with smoke, which caused the alarm to go off and 911 calls by neighbors summoned the firefighters.

The managers of his place were alerted in time to bring keys to open the door, to let the firemen in. *The metal cooking pot had melted, but miraculously the fire and the 500 degree heat was confined to that small 8 inch coil, nothing else burned—no fire in the wooden structures. Everything was protected by the powerful hand of God, His furniture in the house, his computers and data, his large screen TVs, his clothes were not touched.* The firemen did not have to use water to control the fire, so no water damage was suffered, only a little smoke in the carpet walls, etc., which was removed with fans.

This reminded him of the powerful hand of protection of God around him and all that he does in this world. In his public speaking engagements he acknowledges God and his presence in him—the source of his talents, genius, and strength.

As the famous scientist Albert Einstein, a great genius correctly pointed out, *Imagination is more important than knowledge and all we can do as human beings is to try and follow God's Thought.*

The Right Stuff Comes In Black

FOURTEEN

Prologue

This book was written to demonstrate unequivocally that any person, regardless of their race, ethnicity, or origin can rise from humble beginnings—be it a poor neighborhood or a place of comfort, if they believe in their creator God Almighty the source of genius and all creativity and themselves—*can rise to the highest level of achievement in any field of endeavor, including engineering, technology, and science.* The only prerequisite, is hard work, focus, and dedication to their God-given talent and their ability to treat others fairly without prejudice as they treat themselves.

It is no small feat to be granted seven U.S. patents in Fiber Optics in six years, impacting the dramatic growth of the Internet globally, several patents pending in Nanotechnology, Cyber security and the environment, two engineering books, and many honors and worldwide recognition, etc., for any individual black or white.

He believes that if one follows Einstein's advice that one should focus on making more progress rather than stopping to listen to accolades, the sky is the limit for any one that strives for excellence. *As Oprah Winfrey said and I quote, "excellence is the best antidote to racism and discrimination."*

The Right Stuff Comes In Black

All people of color may encounter sometimes bizarre and racist treatment along the way because when asked why he always dresses impeccably sometimes in a suit, Dr. Mensah used the following encounter to explain this habit. He was in an elevator in a very nice and expensive hotel in downtown St. Louis dressed in jeans going to get breakfast prior to making an important speech in one of the largest sold out auditoriums in the city. An older lady asked him to make sure her room is cleaned in an hour, to which he replied, "I do not work here, I am just a hotel guest like you going to breakfast." She obviously started apologizing for her behavior and attitude. In her mind, a black person cannot stay in a fancy hotel *like this one in the South and that all blacks she meets on the top VIP floors* are workers in the hotel. The irony is that the hotel was actually owned by a black person. He said he was probably smarter than anyone in her family.

Oprah Winfrey was shopping in Switzerland for a handbag during a recent trip, and the young white sales attendant in the store will not show the handbag to her, saying Oprah could not afford this expensive item. Oprah made enough money that year to buy the entire store, but was prejudged by this attendant because of her skin color.

There are other encounters like this including Bob Johnson getting into his Jaguar dressed down at a Four Seasons Hotel, and an older lady getting in the backseat requesting that she should be driven to the mall, thinking Bob was the chauffeur. Hopefully with the creation of his World Success Park as people and visitors of all races get exposed to the successes of different races, they will respect each other and act according to what Dr. King said, "Judgments based not on one's skin color but on the content of one's character." *The World Success Park can bring peace respect, and understanding among the human race.*

America is a great country and will continue to be great as long as it is using all the talents of its people unlike other countries that do not have people from all races, the proverbial melting pot. America is the also the land of great opportunity. God bless America.

Appendix A

Two of the Seven Patents Awarded to Dr. Mensah

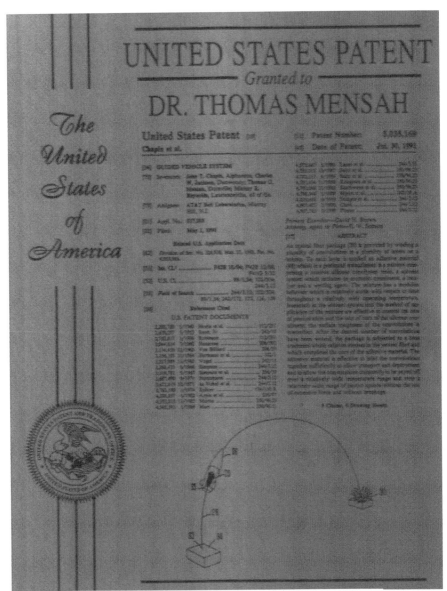

**FIBER OPTIC GUIDED VEHICLE PATENT
(FOG-M MISSLE)**

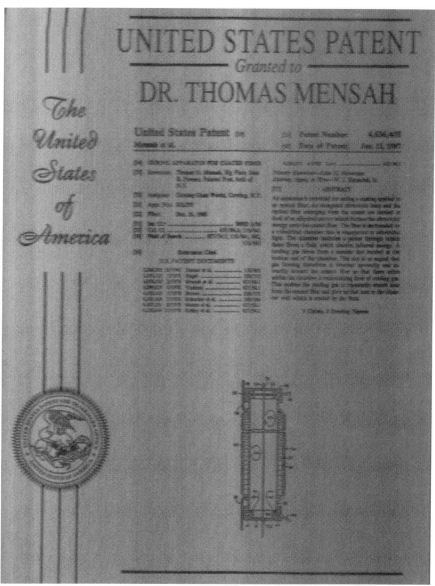

**FIBER OPTIC MANUFACTURING PATENT
(UV CURING SYSTEM)**

REFERENCES:

1 Ebony Magazine Inc, October 2006.

2. Chemical Engineering Progress Magazine, October 2008.

3. Aerospace America, January 2012.

4. Georgia Institute of Technology Annual report on Research, 2005.

5. Chemical Engineering Progress Magazine, October 2008.

6. Bloomberg Business News, Digital West May 9 2013.

7. MIT Visiting Committee Members Booklet, 1988-1992.

8. Aerospace America, AIAA Monthly Magazine, October 2012.

9. T.O. Mensah, et al US Patent No. 5,064,490, Methods of providing an Optical Fiber Package, 1992.

10. T. O Mensah et al, US Patent No. 4,955,688, Optical Fiber Package and Methods of Making, 1992.

11. T. O Mensah et al, US Patent No. 4,792,347, Method of coating Optical Waveguide Fiber, 1987.

12. T. O. Mensah et al, US Patent No. 4,692,615, Apparatus for Monitoring Tension in a Moving Fiber using Fast Fourier Transform Analysis., 1987.

13. T. O. Mensah et al, US Patent No. 4,531,959, Method and Apparatus for coating optical Fibers, 1985.

14. T.O. Mensah et al, US Patent No. 4,636,405 , Curing Apparatus for coated Fiber, 1987.

15. T.O. Mensah et al, Radiation Effects on Optical Fibers, Proceedings of European Conference on Optical Fibers, ECOC, Helsinki, 1987.

16. T. O. Mensah; Enhancement of Strauss Mixing in High Speed Thin film Reactors,Chemical Engineering Communication Journal, 1984.

17. T. O. Mensah, K. Gramoll, Finite Element Analysis of composite overwrap structures, US Army workshop proceedings, New Orleans, September 1994.

18. T. O. Mensah, P. Boatner, A. Erbil, Optical properties of Epitaxial PLT Thin Films, Proceedings of Materials Research Society, Annual Conference, Boston, 1995.

19. T.O. Mensah: Superconductor Engineering Book AIChE Series; ISBN 0816905673.

20. T.O. Mensah , P. Naramsimham; Fiber Optics Engineering Book, ISBN 0816904189.

21. T. Mensah, P. Ruffin, et al; Nano-based Materials for use in Missile Sub-systems and Components, Proceedings of AIAA Weapons Effectiveness Conference, Monterey, CA Jan 2012.

22 T.O. Mensah, J. Koo , CRASTE Proceeding Commercial Access to Space, Atlanta, October 27, 2012.

23. T.O. . Mensah et al US Patent No. 5,035,169, Guided Vehicle System, 1990.

24. T. O. Mensah, Invited Speaker, United Nations Energy Forum, September 2009.

25. T.O. Mensah, Invited Speaker Columbia University Seminar, Knowledge, Technology, and Social Systems.: Impact of Fiber Optics A Key Enabling Technology for the 21st Century, March 2012.

26 T.O. Mensah, Fiber Optic Tethered Robots for Video Imaging of the Gulf Oil Repair, Several Thousand feet below the Sea Surface: The Eminent Engineers Forum, Annual Meeting American Institute of Chemical Engineers, Salt Lake Utah, 2011.

27. T.O. Mensah, Plenary Lecture, Nanotechology Applications in the US Smart Grid Infrastructure: Annual Meeting, American Institute of Chemical Engineers, Salt Lake,Utah, 2011.

28. S. Ramachandran, A. Willner et al, June 28 Issue, The Journal of Science, 2013.

29. Keynote Speech in South Africa by United States President Barack Obama: Electricity Development Assistance for Africa, June 2013.

30. T.O. Mensah, Editor in Chief; Frontiers of Nanotechnology, Advanced Commercialization of Products and Processes in press AIChE and Wiley Publishing, New York.

31. T.O. Mensah, Lecture and Presentation; The Future of the Internet, American Institute of Aeronautics and Astronautics Meeting, Georgia Institute of Technology, Atlanta, Georgia, September 17, 2013.

Proof

Made in the USA
Charleston, SC
14 August 2014